THE ROLE OF ADULT GUIDANCE AND EMPLOYMENT COUNSELLING IN A CHANGING LABOUR MARKET

EF/96/40/EN

Biographical note

This report has been compiled by Glenys Watt, Director of Blake Stevenson Ltd. Glenys Watt has been the technical co-ordinator for the Eurocounsel programme since its inception in 1991, and prior to that undertook the research for the feasability study.

Blake Stevenson Ltd. is a research and consultancy company which specialises in social and economic development with a particular focus on issues relating to employment and unemployment.

Blake Stevenson Limited, 12/A Cumberland Street, South East Lane,
Edinburgh EH3 6RU, Scotland.
Tel: (+44) 131.558.3001 Fax: (+44) 131.556.3422
Directors: Glenys Watt and Norma Hurley
Registered in Scotland No. 140770

THE ROLE OF ADULT GUIDANCE AND EMPLOYMENT COUNSELLING IN A CHANGING LABOUR MARKET

Glenys Watt
Blake Stevenson Limited

**Final Report on EUROCOUNSEL:
An Action Research Programme on
Counselling and Long-Term
Unemployment**

European Foundation
for the Improvement of Living and Working Conditions
Wyattville Road, Loughlinstown, Co. Dublin, Ireland
Tel: +353 1 204 3100 Fax: +353 1 282 6456
Email: postmaster@eurofound.ie

Cataloguing data can be found at the end of this publication

Luxembourg: Office for Official Publications of the European Communities, 1996

ISBN 92-827-8279-4

© European Foundation for the Improvement of Living and Working Conditions, 1996

For rights of translation or reproduction, applications should be made to the Director, European Foundation for the Improvement of Living and Working Conditions, Wyattville Road, Loughlinstown, Co. Dublin, Ireland.

Printed in Ireland

PREFACE

This report brings together the findings of an action research programme EUROCOUNSEL, initiated by the Foundation in 1991. The aim of this programme has been, through an interactive process of research and exchange of information and experience, to identify ways to develop and improve the quality and effectiveness of employment counselling and adult guidance services. Their role in preventing and resolving the problem of long-term unemployment is increasingly being recognised and the past five years have seen considerable growth in the number and complexity of these services across the European Union. In some areas, however, such services are either unavailable or not very developed and there is still a greater reliance on passive labour market measures.

The first phase of the Eurocounsel programme involved research in 10 local labour market areas in six Member States (Denmark, Germany, Ireland, Italy, Spain and the United Kingdom). The first aim was to assess existing services and their effectiveness at their delivery point - the local level. This work included active contacts with the main actors - public authorities, trade unions, employers, users and providers of services.

The second phase of the programme examined the role of employment counselling in the light of rising unemployment and increasing pressure on public resources. It defined the key elements of good practice in labour market counselling and developed a cross-national exchange of information and experience through a major European conference, a seminar for senior government officials and a small programme of study visits for counselling practitioners.

The third and final phase of the programme has sought to look forward at the role of employment counselling and guidance for adults in the changing labour market of the 1990's and beyond. High unemployment, especially of a long duration, persists in many regions of Europe. European employment policy has been developed and strengthened through the European Council meetings of Essen, Cannes, Madrid and Florence. A comprehensive and integrated strategy has been elaborated to stimulate job growth and improve economic performance and competitiveness. The European Council has re-affirmed that the fight against unemployment and for equal opportunities is the priority task for the Community and its Member States. Key elements in this fight are the improvement of labour market policy including the development of "active" policies and the strengthening of measures to help the most disadvantaged groups in the labour market.

It is in this context that the report aims to make a contribution to policy development. In a more precarious and flexible labour market, the need for support to deal with:- transitions into and out of the labour market; job and occupational mobility; periods of unemployment and the need for training and life-long learning, becomes increasingly apparent. The demand for adult vocational guidance and employment counselling is growing both from individuals seeking work and developing their careers and from those seeking to improve the management of the labour force and to reduce economic and social exclusion. This report looks at the implications of these changes for existing services and, in particular, examines two issues which the Eurocounsel programme had earlier identified as important for service improvement: the development of linkages between service providers and with other labour market organizations; and the measurement and evaluation of counselling services as regards both their quality and their effectiveness.

On 7 December 1995 this report was evaluated by representatives of the Foundation's Administrative Board. This group has acted as an Advisory Committee throughout the programme (see Appendix 1) providing a valued input from the viewpoint and experience of policy makers and advisors. The report was approved subject to minor modifications. While clarifying that the final recommendations were the responsibility of the author, the Committee expressed its continued support for the work undertaken and the contribution it brought to a better understanding of the role of employment counselling and guidance for adults and of ways to improve its quality and effectiveness. Its role in prevention was of particular significance especially in a more flexible and fragmented labour market. While being no panacea for unemployment these services had the potential to offer considerable support to many different groups experiencing problems in the labour market. They can play an important role in re-insertion and in the fight against exclusion.

The Foundation wishes to thank Glenys Watt and the authors of the national reports for their active participation in the Eurocounsel programme and the members of the Advisory Committee for their support and guidance.

Clive Purkiss
Director

Eric Verborgh
Deputy Director

TABLE OF CONTENTS

Page

1	INTRODUCTION	1

2 WHY EUROPE NEEDS GOOD QUALITY LABOUR MARKET COUNSELLING AND GUIDANCE

2.1	Job creation is the priority	7
2.2	Unemployment and long-term unemployment	10
2.3	Social exclusion linked to economic exclusion	13
2.4	The rapidity of change in our society	15
2.5	The response to these challenges	20
2.6	The developing role of counselling at European level	22
2.7	Conclusion	29

3 WHAT IS COUNSELLING?

3.1	Introduction	31
3.2	Definitions	31
3.3	Types of counselling activity	32
3.4	Who provides counselling services?	35
3.5	Methods used	44
3.6	The functions of counselling	46
3.7	Target groups	51
3.8	The counselling practitioner	53

		Page
3.9	The potential benefits of counselling	57
3.10	The attributes of "good" counselling	58
3.11	Conclusion	60

4 HOW IS COUNSELLING DEVELOPING TO MEET THE NEEDS OF THE CHANGING LABOUR MARKET?

4.1	Introduction	61
4.2	The evolving role of counselling services	61
4.3	The role of employers	66
4.4	The role of trade unions	68
4.5	The role of users	69
4.6	The role of counselling linked to changes in the labour market	71
4.7	Linkages	87
4.8	The measurement of the quality and effectiveness of counselling	106

5 OVERALL CONCLUSIONS

5.1	Introduction	121
5.2	Employment growth	122
5.3	Local labour market information	124

		Page
5.4	Long-term unemployment	124
5.5	Social exclusion	126
5.6	Active citizenship	127
5.7	The comprehensive counselling system	127
5.8	Training	129
5.9	Centralisation versus decentralisation	130
5.10	Planning counselling services	132
5.11	Linkages	132
5.12	The Market for counselling	134
5.13	Involvement of users	135
5.14	The use of new technology	137
5.15	Measurement and evaluation	138
5.16	Resources	139
5.17	The additional outcomes of action research	139
5.18	Conclusions	141

6 RECOMMENDATIONS

6.1	Summary	143
6.2	European level	146
6.3	National level	153
6.4	Regional and local levels	159
6.5	Conclusion	164

APPENDICES:

Appendix 1: The Eurocounsel Team and Advisory Committee — 167

Appendix 2: References - denoted in text by superscript numbering — 171

Appendix 3: Definitions — 181

Appendix 4: Results of the action element of the Eurocounsel programme — 185

Appendix 5: Recommendations for regional and local strategies — 189

LIST OF TABLES

Table 1: Expenditure on labour market policies, 1992 (% GDP) — 24

Table 2: Basic providers of counselling services in the participating countries in Eurocounsel — 39

Table 3: Groups included in targeting preventive work. — 48

LIST OF FIGURES

Figure 1:   Unemployment Rates in the EU 1970-1995   11

Figure 2:   Unemployment and Long-term Unemployment in the EU, 1985-1994   12

Figure 3:   Percentage of lone parent families with at least one child under the age of 15   16

Figure 4:   Part-time male employment as a % of full-time male employment, and part-time female employment as a % of full-time female employment   18

Figure 5:   Economic and Employment Growth, 1970-1992   21

1 INTRODUCTION

The European Foundation for the Improvement of Living and Working Conditions is concerned with promoting the planning and establishment of a better quality of life for the citizens of the European Union. It is concerned with both the economic and social dimensions of the European Union. Its own Administrative Board reflects this dual purpose as it includes the social partners, employers and trade unions, as well as government officials and representatives from the European Commission. Increasingly too the Foundation has developed contacts with the non-government sector at European and national levels. The European Commission's White Paper on Social Policy (July 1994)[25] recognised the important role which the Foundation has to play

"in analysing the key developments and factors of change concerning living and working conditions in the Union. ...taking account of its tripartite structure [the Foundation] can play an essential role in the dissemination of information and exchanges of experience."

One main focus of the work undertaken by the Foundation over the past ten years has been ways of promoting social cohesion threatened by unpredictable economic and social change. This focus has included research into locally based responses to long-term unemployment, the role of public welfare services, new forms of work and activity, mobility and social cohesion and the Eurocounsel programme. The last of the these, which began in 1991 has as its aim:

"to develop and improve counselling and guidance services for the long-term unemployed and those at risk of becoming so."

This aim includes the development of such services where they do not already exist. Over the five years since the programme was first conceived there has been increasing recognition by a number of organisations concerned with labour market efficiency and effectiveness of the importance of guidance and counselling as an active labour market measure. Indeed the latest OECD Employment Outlook (1995) sets as a "reasonable target", one hour per month of individual counselling for each unemployed person which would entail employing at least one qualified counsellor for each 100 unemployed persons.[34] This is clearly a long-term goal to be aimed for.

The Eurocounsel programme began in May 1991. A three phase programme of work has now been completed. The first phase was concerned with mapping the provision of counselling services, opening up debate and identifying key issues in ten local labour market areas in six countries. At the same time this close examination of local provision was enhanced by consideration of the national context and trends relating to counselling in each of the participating countries. The second phase looked at European developments in this area and identified examples of good practice. The programme has already given rise to a series of publications and these are listed in Appendix 2 of this report. The third and final phase of Eurocounsel has been concerned with the examination in more detail of some key issues identified during the course of the programme. The aim throughout has been to examine how relevant the current provision of counselling services is to the labour market context of the late 1990s and early 21st century.

The Eurocounsel programme has been one of action research. It has sought to involve practitioners and policy makers throughout the process of the research programme so that there have been direct benefits for those concerned. This involvement has taken place at local, national and European levels. Because of this action research focus the programme has had a wider impact than the average more academically oriented research programme. Some of the action results of the programme are illustrated in Appendix 4 of this report.

A total of nine countries have been involved in Eurocounsel. Six of these have been involved from the beginning (Denmark, Germany, Ireland, Italy, Spain and the UK); Austria was involved in Phase 2 of the programme and France and the Netherlands have participated in Phase 3. This has allowed the programme to work on the basis of a wide understanding of the different kinds of counselling available throughout the European Union. This understanding has been enhanced by close involvement of other institutions involved in this subject area, in particular the European Commission, CEDEFOP, the OECD and the ILO. Representatives from these different organisations have attended the Advisory Committee meetings of the Eurocounsel programme, together with representatives from the social partners, which has enabled it to draw on their collective expertise. (A list of those who have been involved in the Advisory Committee is contained in Appendix 1).

This document is the final report of the Eurocounsel programme. It is addressed mainly to policy makers at national and European levels in the hope that the issues raised will stimulate further discussion and action and promote recognition of the need for such services to be improved. The report seeks to explore the complex issues which have been raised during the course of the research programme and to make recommendations as to the future provision of such services. In particular it poses questions and provides examples as to how such services can help to address the problem of unemployment and long-term unemployment, seeks to analyse the ways in which the effectiveness of such services can be measured and improved and asks what role counselling and guidance services should and must play in the labour market of the late 1990s and beyond.

Chapter 2 sets the economic and social context within which counselling related to the labour market is taking place at European level. It explains why Europe needs good labour market counselling and guidance.

Chapter 3 provides background information on what is meant by counselling and explores some of the key general issues relating to its provision.

Chapter 4 examines how counselling is being provided and where the gaps exist. It provides the results of the three research topics which have been explored in greater depth during the final phase of the programme: the role of counselling in a changing and flexible labour market; linkages between counselling providers and with other agencies concerned with the labour market; and the measurement of the quality and effectiveness of counselling services and provision.

Chapter 5 draws the final conclusions from the Eurocounsel programme.

Chapter 6 makes recommendations for the future development of counselling services at European and national levels so that they can meet the needs of the changing labour market of the late 1990s and early 21st century.

2 WHY EUROPE NEEDS GOOD QUALITY LABOUR MARKET COUNSELLING AND GUIDANCE

2.1 Job creation is the priority

Although there are indications from recent OECD and EU labour market reports that the economic recovery is now well established after the slump of the early 1990s, there is still widespread concern in Europe at the lack of employment growth. The European Commission's seminal document on this subject, the White Paper, "Growth, Competitiveness and Employment" (December 1993) set out clearly the problems of economic growth without a corresponding rise in employment, so-called "jobless growth", and stressed the need within Europe to find new ways to create and stimulate job growth.[35] It proposed an action plan (known as the "Delors Plan") with the aim to create 15 million jobs by the year 2000 (equivalent to around 5% employment growth). Its six priorities for action on jobs are:

- lifelong training and learning;
- greater flexibility in businesses, both internally and externally;
- greater expectations from decentralisation and initiative taking;
- a reduction in the relative costs of low qualified work;
- a thorough overhaul of employment policies; and
- efforts to meet new needs which may create jobs.

Meeting in December 1994, the Essen Summit of the European Council[36] reinforced the Delors Plan and the importance attached by the European Union to this whole problem of structural unemployment:

"The fight against unemployment and the promotion of equality of opportunity for men and women will continue in the future to remain the paramount tasks of the European Union and its Member States."

It proposed five priorities for action to solve the problems:

- investment in vocational training;
- increasing the employment-intensiveness of growth by:
    - more flexible organisation of work;
    - wage agreements below the level of productivity so that further job creation is encouraged;
    - promotion of initiatives linked to new requirements such as the environmental and social spheres.
- reduction of non-wage labour costs;
- improving the effectiveness of labour market policy;
    (in particular this suggests the need to move from passive to active labour market policies)
- improving measures to help groups which are particularly hard hit by unemployment: in particular young people (especially school leavers who have virtually no qualifications), women, older workers and the varied groups of the long-term unemployed who have a range of different requirements.

> *"...The fight against long-term unemployment must be a major aspect of labour market policy. Varying labour market policy measures are necessary according to the very varied groups and requirements of the long-term unemployed"*

The recommendations need to be taken further than this in order to emphasize the actions which are required to prevent long-term unemployment and protect people from the increasingly flexible, and precarious, labour market. For example the labour market requires that people are constantly re-skilling and there are sound economic arguments for this in that it can assist in keeping welfare costs down and in raising competitiveness. This need for renewal and updating of skills relates to the lifelong learning approach which is being promoted in 1996 through the Year for Lifelong Learning. In order to foster this continual learning process, people require more access to advice, information and counselling services throughout their lives. This issue of the role which counselling can play to equip people with the tools they will need to handle the various transitions in their working lives will be examined further in this report.

The Essen Summit urged individual Member States to adapt these recommendations to their own economic and social situation by drawing up multi-annual programmes to address the issues. It set the agenda clearly in relation to job creation as the top priority. What is the background in Europe to this focus on the urgency of job creation?

2.2 Unemployment and Long-term unemployment

Since the early 1970s and the first major oil crisis the European economy has been marked by a series of recessions and recoveries. Full employment, which was regarded almost as a right in the 1960s, has gradually been eroded and there are now countries which have openly abandoned this as a stated goal (for example Denmark). Instead new goals have and are being developed which include the "activation" of citizens to take up a range of paid and unpaid activities, greater emphasis on human resource development and increased assistance with the many transitions into, between and out of working life. Although there have been recoveries, and since 1994 it appears that most European countries are enjoying one after the latest recession of the early 1990s, it has become clear that the underlying trend for unemployment has been upwards and that there is a problem of structural as well as cyclical unemployment. Figure 1 illustrates this problem.

Figure 1

Unemployment Rates in the EU 1970-1994

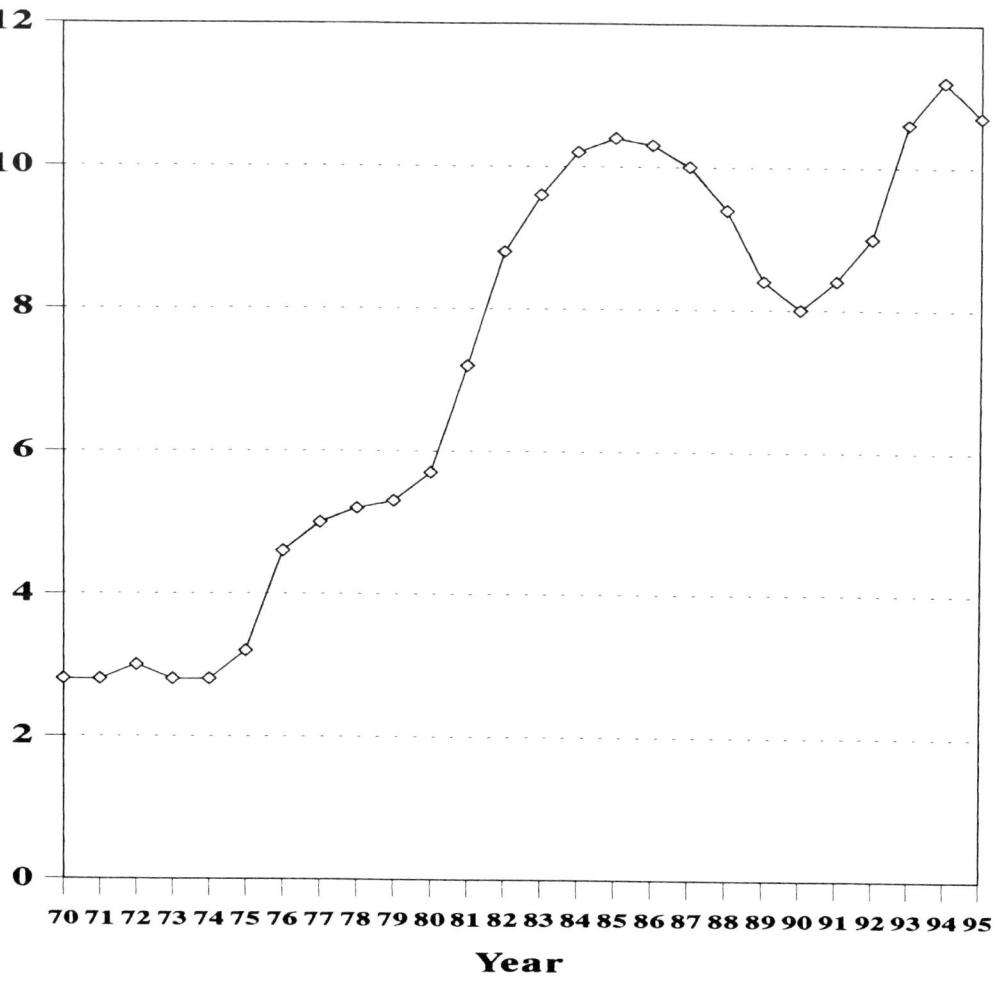

Source: EUROSTAT

Within the numbers of unemployed one of the more worrying trends is that even when unemployment does begin to fall long-term unemployment remains high. Long-term unemployment does not fall in relation to the level at which the unemployment rate falls. This trend is particularly important for those with responsibility for the planning and provision of counselling services. It would appear to place even greater emphasis on the need for preventive counselling (see Chapter 3 of this report).

Figure 2

Unemployment and Long-term Unemployment in the EU, 1985-1994

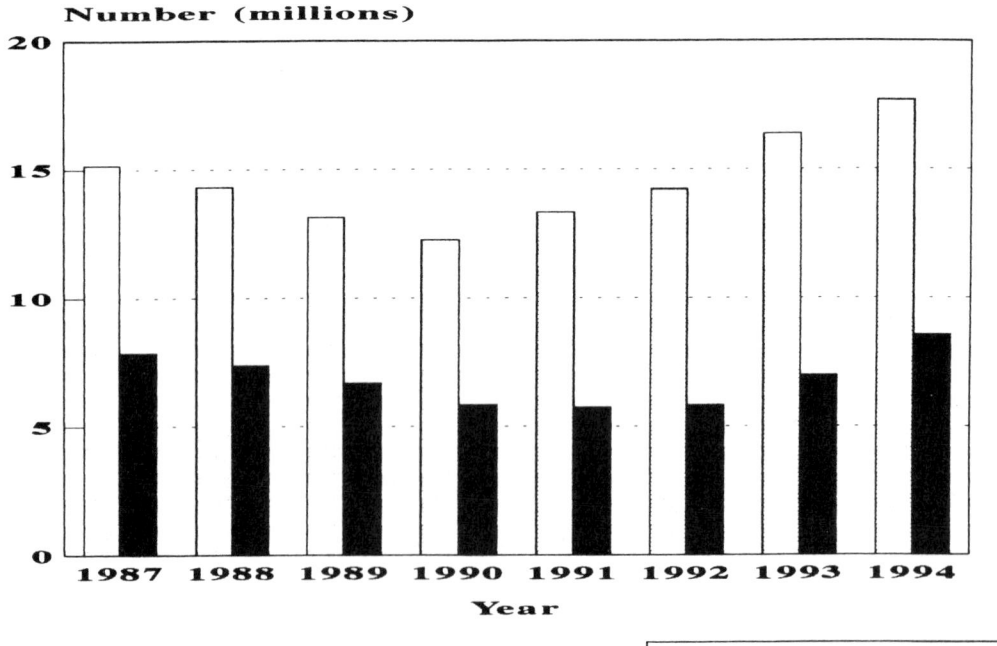

Source: EUROSTAT

Until recently in Europe, the macro-economic response to this problem of unemployment has been focused on fiscal and economic issues such as keeping a low level of inflation rather than on employment growth per se. The main aim during the 1980s and early 1990s was the liberalisation of markets so that goods, services and people could move more freely. Economic integration within the Union was seen as the key to economic and employment growth. However the White Paper mentioned at the start of this chapter analysed clearly that economic growth could and does exist without a corresponding growth in employment. This has led to the increasing emphasis on job creation illustrated by the outcomes of the Essen Summit. Another of the reasons why this concern over the lack of employment growth has arisen is due to the recognition that there are potentially severe societal dangers if an "underclass" of those who are economically excluded from society is allowed to persist and grow.

2.3 Social exclusion linked to economic exclusion

The Treaty on European Union, ratified at the end of 1993, defines economic and social cohesion as one of the primary commitments of the Union. The fear which continuing high levels of unemployment and long-term unemployment gives rise to is that economic exclusion from jobs and work will be accompanied for many people by social exclusion and that this may lead to a breakdown in the kind of society to which Europe aspires. The issue of social exclusion has risen, alongside that of unemployment, to take a high place on the European agenda. The

White Paper on European Social Policy (July 1994) includes detailed proposals for further intervention in the labour market, including targets for basic skills, a job guarantee for all under 18s, a revival of apprenticeships and better information and consultation of employees.[25] The White Paper has been reinforced by the publication of the Medium Term Social Action Programme (1995-1997).[37] This document states that the creation of jobs remains the priority and declares that

"A new balance must be achieved between the economic and social dimensions, in which they are treated as mutually reinforcing, rather than conflicting, objectives."

The Social Chapter of the Maastricht Treaty is an example of an attempt by most of the countries in the EU to achieve a balance between the economic and social dimensions of the active labour market by, for example, restricting the number of hours people are allowed to work, and addressing issues of child and family responsibility.

Businesses themselves are recognising the strong economic arguments for their involvement in tackling unemployment and social exclusion. This link between their own economic concerns and wider social issues is illustrated by the European Declaration of Businesses Against Exclusion which outlines the kinds of actions which businesses can take to assist in combating exclusion either within their own work places or in the surrounding community. [39]

At European level trade unions too are concerned with the issue of social exclusion. A recent document produced by the European Trade

Union Confederation sees trade unions responding to this challenge in collaboration with other organisations and states that in tackling this issue trade unions are returning to their original raison d'etre. The document is the result of research on the situation regarding social exclusion in different countries and what the trade unions see as their response to it. It proposes a programme of action to tackle the issues of poverty and exclusion.[27]

2.4 The rapidity of change in our society

The problems of exclusion are not only linked to unemployment. There are a whole range of complex factors which may increase rather than decrease the likelihood both of economic and social exclusion. We are involved in a period of rapid change which has been likened to that of the Industrial Revolution in north European countries in the late eighteenth and early nineteenth centuries.

2.4.1 Demographic changes

The factors of change have been well documented.[38] They include demographic changes as well as institutional and technological changes. One of the key demographic changes is that in Europe our society is ageing. It is estimated that by the year 2010 over a quarter of those living in the European Union will have celebrated their 60th birthday. This trend towards an ageing population will lead to what has been termed the "pensions crisis": how will the State support such large numbers of people who are economically inactive, in particular when the numbers of those who are economically active are set to decline?

There are also changes in the structure of families. Divorce rates are higher in many European countries than twenty years ago and there is an increase in the proportion of lone parent families with at least one child under 15 (Figure 3). With increasing numbers of women entering the labour market there are pressures on service provision for child-care and other dependants. These demographic changes amount to a social upheaval.

Figure 3

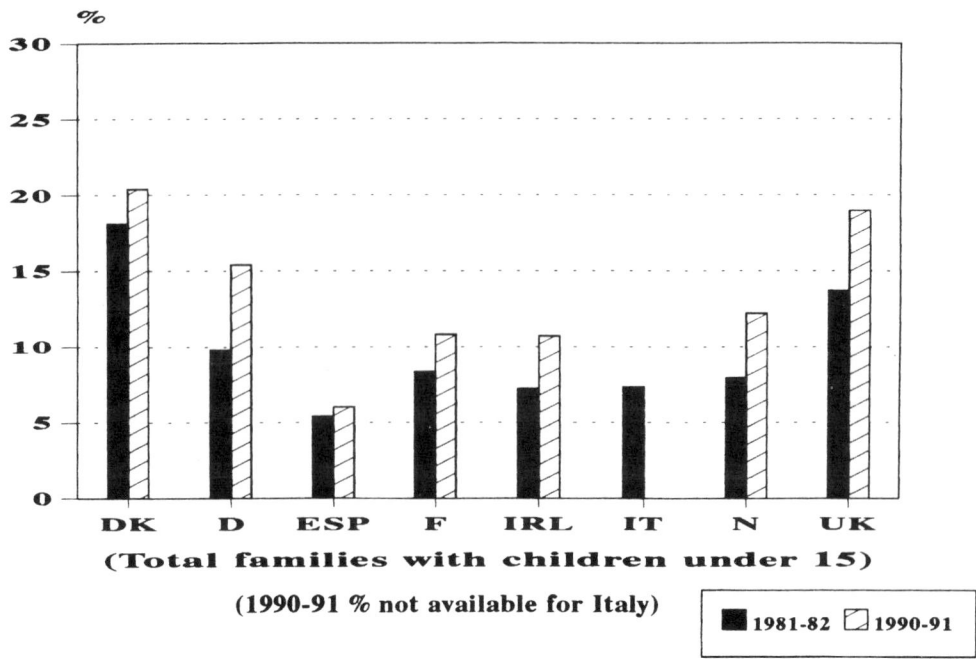

Percentage of lone-parent families with at least one child aged under 15

(Total families with children under 15)

(1990-91 % not available for Italy) ■ 1981-82 ☐ 1990-91

Source: EUROSTAT

2.4.2 Technological change

The changes being brought about by the introduction of new technologies will affect every aspect of our lives. The potential for improved service provision and communications is only beginning to be realised. On the negative side it is feared that while the advent of the Information Society may bring many benefits in terms of access to educational opportunities and information about services generally, it will also increase the possibilities of exclusion of those who for whatever reason cannot have access to it. In relation to direct job creation the balance between the destruction of jobs in the shorter term will have to be set against the potential of job creation in the longer term. There is particular concern in relation to job losses for middle-aged people, over the age of 45. This group in turn is one of those most at risk in terms of long-term unemployment and there is a need for specific assistance and job creation activities for this age group.

2.4.3 Institutional and work changes

In the world of work there are clear institutional and organisational changes taking place. The trend is towards flatter and less hierarchical structures: there have been many redundancies in the ranks of middle management as these changes take effect. Leaner structures also encourage organisations to make more use of flexible labour to handle times of extra demand for their goods or services. This has led to an increase in part-time working, temporary and short-term contracts. This is just one way in which the world of work is changing. The writer Charles Handy in his book *The Age of Unreason*[28] questions whether we should even continue to use the word "employment". Certainly there are fundamental changes to employment as it has been known since the Industrial Revolution: the norm of 50 hours a week for 50 weeks a year for 50 years of a working *man's* life has disappeared. Hours have been reduced, many people work in part-time employment, large numbers of women have entered the labour force and job insecurity is common for many employees at all levels and in all sectors.

Figure 4

Part-time male employment as a % of full-time male employment, and part-time female employment as a % of full-time female employment

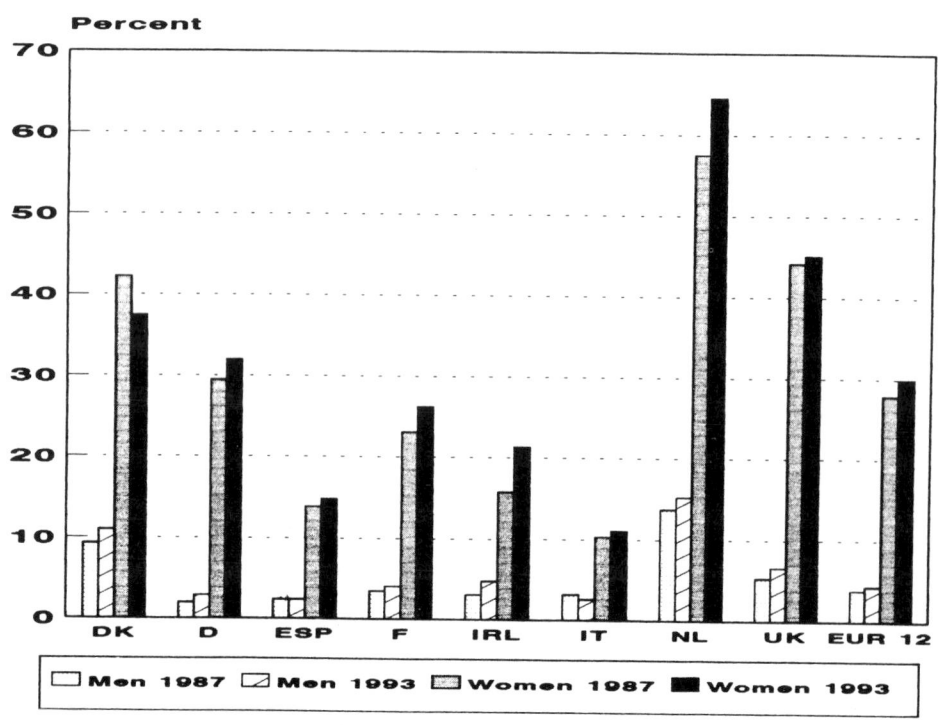

Source: EUROSTAT Yearbook, 1995

2.4.4 Future labour market trends

Future labour market trends would suggest that these changes will increase rather than decrease. The labour market in twenty to thirty years' time will be significantly different. New technology will allow faster and easier communications so that the global market place will become even more of a reality. More people will work on temporary contracts and what we currently perceive as "part-time" jobs. There will be a general reduction in working hours and more people will work on annualised working time. More people will hold several "jobs" at once and flexibility will be an essential prerequisite for many of these short-term contracts. At the same time as this increase in flexibility it is likely that there will be less protection for workers and an overall greater sense of insecurity. There will be many more skilled jobs and many of these will be in small and medium sized enterprises: as Handy[28] states, rather than having complex organisations with straightforward jobs there will be "simplified organisations with complex jobs". Those without the education and skills to compete in this new information led labour market will be liable to hold lower paid service jobs or to remain unemployed. Jobs in some industries, for example agriculture, will continue to decline whilst there will be growth in other sectors such as the environment.

To sum up there will be a great increase in labour market transitions and every time this happens there will be a risk of unemployment and long-term unemployment. The importance of lifelong learning emerges clearly from this scenario. There is concern that this future world of work will increase rather than decrease the risks of social exclusion. What is clear is that the role of counselling and guidance will be increasingly important given these changes and the pressing need which everyone will have to be involved in lifelong learning and to adapt to labour market and indeed leisure time requirements.

2.5 The response to these challenges

The challenge within Europe, and globally, is to acknowledge the changes which have and are occurring and to re-define the kind of society we can build given the new economic and social parameters. As the report of the European Anti-Poverty Working group on Combating Social Exclusion in the European Union (1995)[29] expresses it:

> *"Economic growth and social progress should be seen as two sides of the same coin. The creation of wealth and ensuring that everyone can share in this wealth are inextricably linked. The costs of unemployment and economic marginalisation are enormous, for the individual, for the state and for society in general."*

In addition to the work already referred to in the Commission's White Paper and at the Essen Summit other organisations have been addressing these issues, in particular the Organisation for Economic Co-operation and Development (OECD) and the International Labour Organisation (ILO). The OECD's Jobs Study 1950-1995 [26] analyses unemployment in the OECD countries for this period and offers its own strategy for improving the situation. The analysis identifies the differences between employment growth in Europe and other industrialised areas. The difference between the EU and the USA is particularly marked where the latter has seen both economic and employment growth. It can be argued however that this growth in employment in the USA has been largely due to the increase in low paid jobs there. Europe has to decide in tackling this crisis whether it wishes to promote a US style of job creation or whether there is another route to solving the problem.

Figure 5

USA and EU Economic and Employment Growth 1970-1992

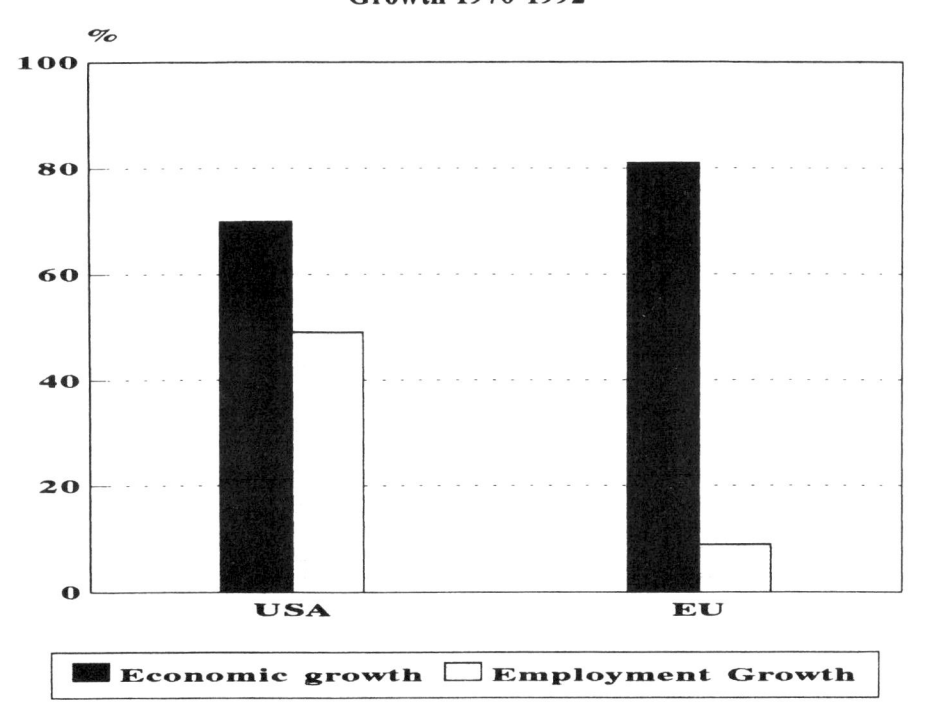

Source: OECD Jobs Study 1993

The ILO prepared a report, World Employment 1995, for the World Summit for Social Development in Copenhagen. (March 1995) The ILO's Director General, Michel Hansenne, argues in the report for an international commitment to full employment in order to provide the basis for international co-operation without which he argues the crisis of unemployment will not be solved. The ILO's focus is not solely on the developed countries but also on those which are developing where it is estimated 95% of the world's 820 million unemployed or underemployed live. [30]

The key strategies to create jobs which emerge from these different sources, the European Commission, the OECD and the ILO revolve around the following:

- the reduction of non-wage labour costs;
- trade liberalisation and promotion of an entrepreneurial climate;
- improved labour force skills through training and education;
- strengthened emphasis on active labour market policies.

2.6 The developing role of counselling at European level

2.6.1 Active versus passive labour market measures

Traditionally Member States of the European Union have spent more on passive labour market measures than on active ones. Passive measures are those which support the individual *in* unemployment, such as unemployment benefit, while active measures aim to help the individual to leave unemployment. Counselling, which includes the provision of information, advice, guidance and in-depth support to help people deal with the increasing complexity and risks inherent within the changing labour market is an active labour market measure which is centrally concerned with risk management.

The historical reasons for the emphasis on passive labour market measures are associated with the post-war goals of full employment and social protection. While employment levels remained high it was possible to support those who were temporarily out of work by funding benefits to give them income. Table 1 demonstrates that this focus on passive measures has remained the predominant approach to tackling unemployment although in one or two of the countries the expenditure difference between active and passive is close. For example, in Germany and Portugal the active measures expenditure is about equal or slightly higher than that on passive measures, although it should be noted that these two countries had relatively low unemployment in 1992. Those countries which spent more on passive labour market measures such as Spain and the UK had relatively high unemployment in that year.

Table 1

Expenditure on labour market policies, 1992 (% GDP)

Active measures

	B	DK	D	GR	E	F	IRL	I	L	NL	P	UK
Public employment services and administration	0.19	0.11	0.24	0.07	0.11	0.13	0.14	na	0.04	0.09	0.09	0.17
Labour market training	0.14	0.40	0.59	0.18	0.08	0.35	0.49	na	0.02	0.21	0.30	0.18
Youth measures	na	0.26	0.06	0.03	0.06	0.23	0.44	na	0.11	0.07	0.38	0.18
Subsidised employment	0.55	0.39	0.52	0.09	0.32	0.11	0.29	na	0.02	0.05	0.04	0.02
Measures for disabled	0.16	0.40	0.24	0.01	na	0.06	0.14	na	0.10	0.63	0.05	0.03
Total expenditure on active labour market policies	**1.04**	**1.56**	**1.65**	**0.38**	**0.57**	**0.88**	**1.50**	**0.80**	**0.29**	**1.04**	**0.86**	**0.58**

Passive measures

	B	DK	D	GR	E	F	IRL	I	L	NL	P	UK
Unemployment compensation	2.07	3.69	1.39	0.79	3.07	1.46	2.89	na	0.25	2.17	0.59	1.69
Early retirement for labour market reasons	0.75	1.28	0.49	na	na	0.47	0.05	na	0.52	na	0.11	na
Total expenditure on active and passive measures	**3.86**	**6.53**	**3.46**	**1.17**	**3.64**	**2.81**	**4.44**	**0.72**	**1.06**	**2.17**	**1.56**	**2.27**

Note: I 1988, B, F, IRL, L, NL 1991, UK 1992-93

Source: OECD

The types of active labour market measures adopted are similar in the different EU countries but there are differences in the emphasis placed on each of them as shown in the levels of expenditure. In the majority of countries a large part of the active measures are concerned with young people and training.

2.6.2 Counselling within European programmes

Counselling has not tended to be regarded as a separate active labour market measure in its own right. It is generally a part of other active labour market measures such as placement and education/training. Many of the European programmes related to the labour market include counselling as an integral part of the activities they are aimed to support and encourage. The European Social Fund (ESF) Objective 3 programme (1995-1999) aims to combat long-term unemployment and aid the integration into working life of young people and other groups at risk of exclusion from the labour market by providing financial support towards the running costs of training, vocational guidance and employment creation projects. The Measure concerned with Vocational Guidance and Counselling, now renamed Choice and Access, allows for the following kinds of activities: pretraining; job preparation courses; basic literacy and numeracy; accreditation of prior learning; core skills; vocational guidance and counselling.

Most of the Community Initiatives dealing with human resource development now also include vocational guidance and counselling within their remit. LEONARDO, (encompassing the former Commett,

Petra, Force and Eurotecnet programmes) is designed to help the labour force adapt to changes in production systems. It is a particularly important programme for employers as much of the funding goes to them directly. It stresses the importance of life-long vocational guidance and counselling in its Vade-mecum. ADAPT is designed to help the labour force respond to changing needs in the labour market. One of its four main areas of action includes the supply of training, counselling and guidance. The counselling and guidance focus is aimed at those workers who are affected by industrial change in different economic sectors, in particular those threatened with unemployment and those working in small and medium sized enterprises.

URBAN aims to find solutions to serious social problems for depressed urban areas by supporting economic and social revitalisation schemes. It includes funding for mobile advisory units.

The EMPLOYMENT initiative, which addresses issues of equal opportunities, marginalisation and also deals with young people, encompasses the former Now, Horizon and Youthstart programmes. It also includes a strong element of support for the development of vocational guidance and counselling. Many of the non-government organisations which run counselling programmes owe their funding to one of these programmes: for example, many of the vocational counselling opportunities for women in the EU have been funded by the NOW initiative.

EURES is the European Employment Services Network which has been established to facilitate the mobility of workers between European states. Its main aim at present is to provide good information on transnational job opportunities and to facilitate this Eurocounsellors have been established in the Member States. It is recognised that this network only deals with a small percentage of the European labour market and that mostly its services will be for those who are more highly skilled. However it is still in the early stages of its development and there may be scope for cross-fertilisation with some of the Community Initiatives described above. For example, at a later date it may be able to facilitate the exchange of good practice and experience relating to labour market issues.

There is growing consensus at European level in favour of a greater role for counselling within active labour market measures. This reinforces the final report for the ERGO 1 programme[31] on long-term unemployment which stated:

" The key to effective re-integration of the unemployed in the labour market is appropriately resourced counselling."

2.6.3. *The developing role of counselling*

The role of counselling related to the labour market was traditionally one of information and careers guidance, in particular for school pupils and leavers. It is interesting to note that in a country which is in the process of establishing employment and occupational counselling for the first time, the Czech Republic, where unemployment is still low, that the emphasis has been on precisely these areas. But in western Europe the growth in unemployment since the 1970s and especially the embedded nature of long-term unemployment, has led to the development of services more focused on unemployed adults. As job insecurity and mobility becomes more widespread, attention is turning also to the development of counselling services for those who are currently in employment, including offering them within the workplace.

"The provision of information and training alone have proved inadequate tools for the successful social and economic integration of the adult population, the heterogeneity of which requires more specialised approaches and more customised tools and techniques..... Vocational counselling has already become the indispensable accompanying measure to most vocational training, information and work placement services."[32]

Member States increasingly recognise the importance of

"..developing a strategy to achieve an all-age guidance service."[105]

This all-age guidance service will be required to address the needs of older as well as younger workers as there is evidence that early retirement masks problems of unemployment in many countries.

2.7 Conclusion

The issues described in this chapter relating to the European context are also those which concern individual countries to a greater or lesser extent. All the countries involved in Eurocounsel have faced change in the early years of the 1990s and see it continuing into the future; all of them face a crisis of unemployment. However there are huge variations at local labour market level, both between countries and within them, in terms of unemployment rates and the kinds of counselling services which are available. In some countries such as Denmark or the UK there is a well established tradition of counselling and guidance services; in others such services are developing (e.g. Ireland) whereas in others they are still in the early stages of recognising the potential of such services (e.g. Spain and Italy).

Given the concern at European level as to how to tackle unemployment and combat social exclusion, the question for the Eurocounsel programme is what role counselling should be playing in relation to all of this and how it can be made effective and give the highest quality service in what it does. At European level there is a need for policy guidelines to address this issue which countries can then adapt to suit their own circumstances (as has happened with the Essen Summit's approach to job creation). The aim of this report is to provide detailed practical advice and policy recommendations as to how this can be done.

3 WHAT IS COUNSELLING?

3.1 Introduction

This chapter of the report seeks to clarify what is meant by counselling in the context of a changing labour market. It describes the different kinds of activity which can be said to constitute counselling, the different locations where counselling takes place and some of the methods commonly used. The functions which counselling serves, the target groups it aims to reach and the role of the counselling practitioner are examined. Finally it looks at the potential benefits counselling can offer and discusses some of the elements attributed to "good" counselling.

3.2 Definitions

For the purposes of the Eurocounsel programme the term "counselling" has been used as a catch-all word to include:

- information giving;
- advice;
- guidance; and
- counselling itself.

For a fuller discussion of these terms and their precise meaning, please see Appendix 3.

3.3 Types of counselling activity

To help clarify the types of counselling situation with which we are concerned in the Eurocounsel programme it may be useful to define the sorts of situations in which counselling takes place. These range across those services which are specifically related to re-integrating unemployed people back into the labour market to those which develop the skills of clients by directing them to the appropriate training or educational course for their needs or are involved in assisting people to deal with their social circumstances. The provision of counselling services is complex: local labour markets vary enormously and clients' needs are also highly variable. Some clients may need little assistance, others will require intensive and prolonged help. It is important that services are able to adapt flexibly to these different needs while at the same time operating in a co-ordinated manner. This highlights the importance of good linkages between service providers and other organisations concerned with the labour market which is covered in further detail in the next chapter of this report. It also points to some of the problems which may be encountered in trying to evaluate such services: the diversity and flexibility which are essential if the different needs of the individual client are to be met, also make the evaluation process more complex (see Chapter 4).

The kinds of situations where counselling is involved include:

Relating to the labour market

- job placement and job search;

- placement on temporary work creation schemes;

- general advice, information and guidance on the labour market and job opportunities;

- advice and counselling on job creation opportunities such as self-employment, social enterprises, and small business development;

- preventive counselling and assistance with those facing redundancy;

- continuing support once an individual has secured a job (which can be particularly important for those who have been long-term unemployed and who are learning the routines and discipline of the work place anew);

- mediation with employers and local economic development agents to encourage provision of jobs for the unemployed;

- support for employers taking on people who have been long-term unemployed.

Relating to personal development

- confidence building;

- assertiveness;

- careers guidance;

- personal development/action planning;

- psychometric testing and other forms of character and skills assessment.

Relating to education/training

- vocational guidance;

- advice and information about specific courses.

Relating to social welfare

- advice on benefits;

- advice/counselling on problems arising from being out of work such as debt counselling, alcoholism, depression etc

- psychological help.

One of the ways in which this notion of counselling for those who are out of work can be summed up is in the phrase "finding a path". All the types of activity associated with employment counselling or adult guidance available to the unemployed are in one way or another connected with helping the unemployed person to find a path or route that is suited to his/her circumstances. There has been a notable increase in many of the countries involved in Eurocounsel in this approach which involves drawing up a tailored plan for the individual, the personal development plan, which enables them to plan their move forward. For some, who are perhaps only recently unemployed, this may mean that they are "job ready" and they can therefore make use of job placement services. For others however they may face such huge debt problems that the first thing they need to do is to find a way to deal with these problems before moving on to consider new forms of activity relating to their prospects of finding a job.

3.4 Who provides counselling services?

The situations in which counselling takes place vary greatly from country to country and will be further described in the next chapter. However these include the following:

- within the formal public employment services;
- as part of claiming benefits;
- as part of a training course;
- as part of a temporary work scheme;

- within non-government organisations covering a range of needs for different target groups;
- provided by specific adult counselling and guidance services, for both the unemployed and the employed, which operate in the open market.

Services provided by the public employment services are going through a period of considerable change in many countries. The monopoly which they enjoyed to provide placement services to the unemployed has recently been withdrawn in countries such as Germany and Spain taking them down a route which other countries have already pursued (UK, France). Despite these changes the public employment services remain in many countries the single most important provider of counselling services to the unemployed.

The provision of counselling linked to the ability to continue to collect benefits has been severely criticised by many who work with the unemployed. There is evidence that counselling services which are offered under this form of compulsion lose their value as they are so resented by the clients as to become invalid. The argument made on the other side however is that for some long-term unemployed people an element of coercion can be beneficial as they may not otherwise be motivated enough by themselves to take action. This is an argument which will continue to be discussed but in general terms it would appear to be the case that to link access to counselling provision directly to eligibility for benefits is less likely to benefit the individual than if the two can be kept separate.

Counselling as part of a vocational training course is perhaps the most commonly found type of counselling location and it is one which tends to offer the best chance of time allocation to the client. The research on vocational counselling for women in Europe mentioned earlier in this chapter found that this kind of counselling, linked to a training course, was the most commonly offered form of service for women. Some courses are wholly concerned with helping their clients "find a route". Others mix imparting skills with some personal development work. It is a useful context in which to locate counselling, if those who offer the counselling have some experience or are qualified to do so: there are some examples where the training provider is required to provide "counselling" where in fact the trainers are all skill teachers rather than counselling practitioners.

The same argument can be used against counselling which takes place linked to temporary work schemes. This has the potential to be of value, as it can be offered to the individual over a period of time, but once again the question as to who will provide the counselling service is raised.

Activities relating to social welfare, such as debt counselling, advice on benefits or help with other problems arising from being out work, tend not to be included in the services offered to those who are unemployed and long-term unemployed in relation to the labour market by labour market counselling providers. And yet it is often impossible for the long-term unemployed person to focus on their route back into work until they have had some help in solving some of their more immediately pressing problems such as debt. Similarly with women who are returning to the labour market having taken some time off to rear a family, the need to resolve child-care problems is often the most important first step they have to take before considering what it is they would like to pursue by way of a future career for themselves. Many of the specially tailored courses for women returners which include a high counselling content have recognised this need, but the more general services offered for example by the public employment services throughout the different Member States tend not to adopt this more holistic approach. From the client's point of view, what is important is that all their needs are met: the development of counselling providers from different agencies working together in one building (e.g. Denmark's "counselling houses", [9] may help to provide a more holistic response.

Non-government organisations have the greatest scope for flexibility and there is a huge range of different kinds of services on offer. These organisations are often funded through national government programmes or through European funding sources such as the European Social Fund Objective 3 programme which specifically promotes vocational counselling under the heading of "Choices and Access" (see Chapter 2). The problem for such organisations is that they may lack access to labour market and other relevant information and to professional training for staff members. They may also be less publicly accountable and although they may be able to target their services on specific groups, this targeting, by its nature, may exclude others in equal need.

Similar flexibility is found in the growing "market" for counselling providers, although the constraint found in these is that they may require the client to pay for the services received, which can discriminate against those who are unemployed unless there is some form of scheme to sponsor their payment for such services.

The relative importance of the above providers varies from country to country. Table 2 demonstrates the complexity and diversity of provision.

Table 2

Germany	Main provider is the Federal Employment Agency with its network of local employment agencies. In the west local authorities and the non-government sector are also providers. In the east, the initial surge of temporary counselling services introduced as one type of employment measure in 1991, has been reduced due to funding problems. Private employment agencies have recently been licensed in the country (August 1994)
Denmark	There is a close link of counselling provision with the very wide range of educational and training institutions in the country. The public employment service also provides services to those who have unemployment insurance through its local employment offices (AF). There is some growth in self-help and self-governing groups providing counselling.

France	France has a range of public sector providers of counselling including the public employment service (ANPE) and many agencies which address the needs of young people. France has a well-developed system of measures relating to counselling for employees, for those facing redundancy and for the unemployed. In December 1993, new employment legislation was introduced to try and simplify what had become a complex system.
Italy	Of the countries involved in Eurocounsel counselling provision is least developed in Italy although some regions, particularly in the north are actively developing services. The public employment service still has the official public monopoly but more local organisations such as the Agenzie per l'Impiego, the Agenzie del Lavoro, the CILOs and the Informagiovani are providing the main counselling services.
Ireland	There is very wide range of providers but there has not been a long tradition of adult guidance as in some other countries in the north of Europe. Providers include the public employment service (FÁS), educational institutions, the local Area Based Partnership companies. A new development which should bring more counselling to the local level is that of the Local Employment Services which are described more fully later in this chapter

Netherlands	The execution of employment policy has been decentralised in the Netherlands and is co-ordinated at regional level by the 28 Regional Employment Boards. These Boards have responsibility for the Employment Exchanges and Vocational Training Centres. The municipalities are also involved in the provision of services to the long-term unemployed. Other agencies, such as private outplacement bureaus and temporary employment agencies, are involved but are limited in number.
Spain	The public employment service, INEM, remains a key provider although its monopoly ended in 1994. Other providers have emerged to meet the needs not being met. Regional authorities now play a significant role. Other services are provided by the administrations at district and local level and by non-government groups. Among the latter are the growing numbers of self-help organisations established by different sections within the unemployed.
UK	There are a plethora of providers in the UK with the public employment service as one of these. The non-government sector is important in the UK for the provision of counselling services. There is increasing emphasis on the opening up of a market for counselling services: for example the Careers Service, formerly run by local education authorities is now offered under contract through competitive tendering on the open market.

Austria	Austria has a wide range of counselling providers including the public employment service and "private" organisations dealing with counselling for unemployed people, people threatened by unemployment, and especially for those who are long-term-unemployed. It is a well-developed system on a regional level. In the last two years the importance of private organisations has been reduced and the focus has been given more to initiatives which combine counselling with training/employment. With the separation of the national employment service from the central administration and its development as an autonomous body, a new impetus in improving the counselling services of the regional public employment department is noticeable.

What is clear from the brief descriptions given in Table 2 is that the public employment services remain as the main or core provider in most countries but that other organisations are required to meet the needs of those who are either not covered by the public employment services or of those who are covered but require more time or more specialised assistance. One of the complaints from practitioners in the public employment services is that they do not have enough time to give to clients and in some countries, for example Germany, such time as they do have is being further eroded due to the pressure on resources and proposed cuts in the number of counselling practitioners. The German Public Services and Transport Trade Union (OTV) has calculated that in future public employment service practitioners will be able to spend only an average three minutes in total with each of their clients.[10] This is a long way from the OECD's target of one hour per month per unemployed person!

Although the public employment services remain important providers there is evidence that the complexity of service provision is if anything increasing rather than decreasing. The removal of the public employment service's monopoly in countries such as Germany and Spain and the growing privatisation of services in many countries (especially the UK) has encouraged this diversity. The positive aspects of such diversity are that it allows for flexibility and breadth in the provision of services, and should mean that most needs can be fulfilled. However the negative aspects are that the increasing complexity makes access to services even more difficult for those seeking them and in some instances may discriminate against the unemployed where charges are made for the services provided. Providers who are operating as private businesses will aim to seek those clients who can pay for what they are receiving and so in some countries, such as the UK and Germany, there appears to be greater interest in providing services for the employed than has previously been the case. Such providers also tend to deal with the less difficult cases amongst the unemployed, in order to boost their success rates if on contract to a state body.

The non-government sector, which in itself is hugely diverse, appears to be the provider which can both be flexible and meet the needs of a wide range of people and at the same time can offer services to those who cannot afford to pay for them. However, the main constraint for non-government providers is the competition for resources as well as clients. This can mean that those who are able to compete best, for example in obtaining European funding, are able to survive while those who do not have such skills or capacity may collapse: an approach based on competition does not ensure that the needs of the most vulnerable groups are being met but rather leaves it to the "market" to determine who will be provided for and there can be dangers in this approach if there is concern to meet the needs of those who are excluded.[11] In Germany the issue of competition at the present time is slightly different: the key focus here is the need to obtain funding through federal model programmes, given the reduction in resources for employment measures in the east. This can lead organisations to design approaches which will obtain funding even though this may not be what is actually needed at local level.[10]

3.5 Methods used

There are many different methods used in the various counselling activities described above. The setting for the provision of counselling services is often on a one-to-one basis but there is significant work undertaken in groups in particular in relation to counselling which is offered as part of a training course. Methods used in group work include role play, discussion, video work. Methods used in either group work or in individual sessions include information packs, active listening, computer programmes (for information dissemination and for assessment purposes) and personal action planning.

Personal action planning (or personal development planning/personal career planning) is a method which has been increasingly used in recent years. Eurocounsel has identified examples of this in all the countries studied [9-14]. It is a method which is open to different interpretations as to exactly what is meant by it. For some counselling agencies it implies helping the user to list the next actions which they are going to take and can be a mechanistic process. For others it is a much more involved process which reflects what counselling, in its purest sense of enabling and empowerment, involves. The process allows the client to reflect on their past experience and achievements and to analyse their strengths and weaknesses. Time is then spent reviewing what the person thinks about their work and education to date before reflecting on what they hope for in the future. Once the person has decided what their future aim is, in relation to work, they can plan how to get there. This may involve, in the first instance, planning what to do about childcare or which qualifications are going to be required in order to equip the client for the work they have in mind. Once this has been done a careful plan will be drawn up which details the steps to be taken and the estimated time it will take to achieve each of these steps. Ideally the Personal Development Plan is a document, and a process, to which the individual can return many times throughout their working lives.

Peer counselling is another method which is being used effectively in some countries. An interesting example of this approach is given in the Case Study Portfolio.[7] A group of unemployed people in Maribo, Denmark were given access to a room in the local employment office (AF) where they could meet and they provided each other with counselling. As with any method there are strengths and weaknesses involved: the key strength is that peer to peer counselling can prove very effective. However, those providing the service require appropriate professional support if they are to be able to maximise this potential effectiveness, or otherwise there is a danger that the services offered will not be of high quality.

The Portfolio contains 21 case studies, from seven countries, which will be of interest to those who wish to know more about the kinds of methods and organisations involved in counselling provision. A Guide to Good Practice in Labour Market Counselling[8] has also been produced and contains suggestions for good practice in counselling procedures.

One of the observations which can be made about this whole area of counselling provision linked to the labour market and to education and training opportunities is that there is a need to agree definitions of what the terms mean. The language used in relation to this subject area is developing all the time and clarity is needed if people are not to become confused as to what is being offered/delivered.

3.6 The functions of counselling

The functions of counselling have been analysed in detail in the earlier Eurocounsel reports.[1 & 2] These have been summarised as including the following:

- prevention;
- solving/matching;
- activation;
- coping.

Prevention is one of the most important functions of the counselling service. Preventive work is undertaken before a person loses their job or as soon after this has happened as possible in order to avoid waiting until the person has become long-term unemployed with all the loss of motivation and confidence which this generally entails. There are some excellent examples of preventive work included in the Portfolio of Case Studies produced by the Eurocounsel programme.[7] One of these is the Austrian Arbeitsstiftung (Labour Foundations) which involve partnerships of the employees, trade unions and employers in helping establish the Foundations which will allow the workers an opportunity to plan for their future and find the right path for their own circumstances. It is interesting to note that similar approaches have been taken in areas facing mass redundancies in certain industries such as the mining industry in the north of the Czech Republic and the same industry in the UK. These examples illustrate the tendency for preventive work to be undertaken in large scale, male-dominated, traditional industries. This raises the question of how smaller businesses, which may be non-unionised, can also be encouraged to engage in preventive work when facing redundancies.

One of the arguments put forward against the use of early preventive counselling is that it could result in a waste of limited resources. It is argued that the majority of people who lose their job will find a new one within a matter of months and that to offer counselling services to such people is wasting them as they do not require this form of assistance. It is therefore necessary to find ways to target assistance at an early stage on those who are likely to be most at risk of falling into long-term unemployment and offering such services to these groups of people as the cost to the state of long-term unemployment is clearly much greater than the cost of such preventive work. Table 3 identifies the kinds of groups who might be included in such targeting of preventive work.

Table 3

High risk groups
Both male and female:
- over 45 years old
- ill health/disability
- ex-offender
- ethnic minority
- low skilled/unskilled/traditional industry skills
- people with limited work experience (i.e. have done same job for whole of working life)
- unskilled youth and school leavers

Solving/matching is the traditional reason why counselling services are provided. It relates to matching the demand for labour from employers with the supply of labour from the potential workforce. This approach works well here there is a high demand for labour and the need is to help those who are seeking jobs to obtain them or equip themselves with the necessary skills to be able to apply for them. There are still many local labour markets in Europe where this approach works well. However as the Eurocounsel programme has shown the high unemployment rates in Europe mean that there are also many local labour market areas where there is low demand for labour and where the counselling practitioner is therefore faced with the task either of helping the person consider moving to an area where their labour will be in demand or to consider other forms of "activation".

"Activation" is a term which relates back to the social employment schemes of the early 1980s which originated in Belgium and the Netherlands. In Denmark, in the 1990s, the ideal of full employment was officially abandoned and instead the government decided to focus on ways to allow more of the population to be active in different ways. This included the introduction of the now well-known job and training rotation scheme, which allows those in work to take leave for education/training and other purposes while the unemployed have the opportunity for real work experience, as well as encouraging people to take up voluntary activities or to opt for part-time work. The aim is to allow as many of the adult population as possible to have some form of meaningful activity in their lives [9]. The activating function of counselling is concerned with all opportunities not directly related to matching/solving the demands of the primary labour market. These include self-employment, social employment such as the Community

Employment scheme in Ireland, voluntary work, training and learning programmes which are pursued for their own sake rather than because they will lead directly to a job in the primary labour market, and employment creation associated with local economic development (which may in time become part of the primary labour market). It can also relate more broadly to the development of "active citizenship", by which is meant the active inclusion of citizens in taking decisions about certain aspects of their living environment which affect them, thus maintaining a role in society for those who may be economically excluded.

The question of what kinds of counselling services to offer in areas where there is low demand for labour has been of particular concern in the Eurocounsel programme and is discussed more fully in the next chapter. For example, in the rural south of Spain there has been a traditionally low demand for labour on the primary labour market. In other parts of the industrialised north (UK, Germany) major traditional industries which used to demand a steady supply of (male) labour, have declined and there are many unemployed, often with out-dated skills. Counselling services are responding to these labour market changes by exploring some of the "activation" ideas described above.

The *coping function* of counselling is one which is understandably unpopular with many practitioners and policy makers as it indicates a sense of passivity and acceptance of the status quo: that this person is going to remain unemployed and therefore must be helped to make the most of the situation in which they find themselves placed. However it is included here as it also the reality for at least some of the long-term unemployed: that their chance of employment in the future is small and that they must be helped to cope with that situation. If this "coping" can be linked to some form of activation as described above then this at least gives a greater sense of inclusion. This will be important for social integration as well as for personal fulfilment. It can be an important service for those who have problems of ill health or who are early retired. It is clearly less acceptable to adopt such a strategy with younger age groups. Most of the passive coping services are in fact provided by social welfare services rather than by those directly concerned with the labour market.

3.7 Target groups

Many services, particularly those offered by non-government organisations, concentrate on specific target groups. As has been mentioned already effort has been made throughout the Member States since the 1980s to target services for women who are returning to the labour market and some of the most innovative, intensive and holistic work on counselling linked to finding routes back into work has been done in this area. Other innovative work has been undertaken with ex-offenders, people with physical and mental disabilities, and young people. Services targeted at the long-term unemployed as a group are found but as always it is essential to remember that this is not a homogeneous group and the different needs of those who find themselves in this position must be addressed.

The converse of those who are targeted is those who are excluded. There are examples of such exclusion from all the countries involved in the Eurocounsel research. Sometimes the exclusion is conscious but more frequently it is just that no-one has thought that here is a group which requires special attention. Immigrants and refugees may find themselves consciously excluded from services in some countries, particularly those who are not legally allowed to work there (although in some countries, for example Denmark, special services aimed at these groups have recently been developed). In Denmark there is exclusion from mainstream labour market services for those who are not members of the employment insurance funds. Other countries have examples of those who are excluded because they do not meet the eligibility criteria for those particular services: for example in many countries a person has to wait a certain amount of time in unemployment before they may access counselling services. This relates to the argument that to target resources on all the newly unemployed is wasteful but on the other hand to wait for twelve months before offering any intensive counselling assistance is too long.

Other groups are excluded because their needs have perhaps not yet been fully realised: for example there are growing numbers of middle-aged men, both low skilled and those who have left middle management positions who are in need of the concentrated assistance which women returners have been able to access over the last decade. Without such assistance they are likely to remain unemployed for a long time and possibly for the rest of their lives. Similarly there are growing numbers of "young-old" who find themselves in early retirement or unemployed through no choice of their own who could be helped to find some active way to contribute to society either through paid part-time work or through voluntary activities. This group is likely to grow as the demographic changes outlined in Chapter 1 occur.

Those who are targeted and those who are excluded varies considerably not just between countries but also within them. The mapping of what services actually exist can help to analyse what services are actually being offered and which groups are being excluded and is a useful tool for policy makers in considering how best to deploy their limited resources.

Self-help groups are one way in which certain groups identify themselves as requiring special attention. There are some interesting examples of this from Spain where there is a group of older unemployed workers, the PM40, an association of unemployed professional workers, and groups for unemployed young people such as the Trinijove Foundation. These associations of the unemployed compete for resources and their strong focus on a particular targeted group can act as an excluding factor for others.

3.8 The counselling practitioner

Just as there are many terms for the activities of counselling so too there are many different names for those who provide the services and they come from a wide range of professional backgrounds. CEDEFOP has undertaken work on the occupational profiles of vocational counsellors[52], which demonstrates this diversity. Counsellors may come from a career guidance background, hold general educational qualifications or come from a psycho-social background. Some become involved in counselling work through other labour market measures such as training.

Eurocounsel has shown that there is a new profession of "labour field counsellors" emerging which combines several of the elements of experience described above. In order to be able to offer services which can help the full development of the client in terms of their career, the educational and training opportunities available to them and the full range of labour market possibilities, such a practitioner has to develop a wide range of skills and abilities. This highly skilled generalist will be a key person in relation to the method increasingly used of personal development planning which involves the highest quality inputs to enable the client to find the appropriate route forward. Of course there will still be a need for specialists who can explore in further depth specific aspects of the client's programme but the case for this high quality generalist is a strong one. The range of skills such a person would require would include:

- ability to access and use information (about the labour market, labour market programmes, educational and training opportunities);

- high level general interpersonal skills;

- networking skills;

- counselling skills;

- activating skills;

- assessment and evaluation;

- knowledge about policy;

- brokerage skills;

- advocacy skills.

This practitioner should also be in a position to analyse and supply feedback to policy makers and providers on the practice involved and on the success of different labour market measures so that they can have a direct input into the development and improvement of services.

One of the skills listed above is that of networking. This is an important skill in an area where there is such a range of providers of labour market services and opportunities and where there is a need to be able to access information and specialist help with ease. Eurocounsel has been particularly concerned to examine the kinds of linkages which are in place and the results of this work will be examined further in Chapter 4 of this report. It appears that networks do exist, especially at informal level between individual practitioners but that the formalisation of networks is less common. One of the reasons given for this is the growing competition between services particularly as many of them are competing for public resources or are operating directly in the open market. Ways have to be sought to promote and encourage networking as it has been shown throughout the Eurocounsel programme to be an essential element of effective services.

One of the stress factors for the counselling practitioner is that they may wish to meet the needs of the client in a manner which goes beyond the objectives of the organisation for which they are working. Many practitioners have spoken of this dilemma. There is no easy solution as the practitioner frequently does not have the time resource to devote to the client. Networking can assist in this if the practitioner is able to refer a client onto someone who is able to give the appropriate help. It is also helpful for the practitioner to receive professional support and supervision but as might be expected in such complex provision of services the opportunity for such professional support varies considerably from country to country and between the different kinds of providers involved. In general it can be said that there is not enough professional support for those who are working in what can be an extremely stressful occupation.

Training for the practitioner has been raised throughout the Eurocounsel programme as an area which requires further attention. The kinds of training which are most appropriate for this "new profession" and who it is to be delivered by are open to discussion. One model which has been described is that of the "open professional model" [33] which makes a positive virtue out of the diversity of skill and backgrounds which are to be found within counselling practitioners. Such an open professional model supplies the basic skills training of counselling but promotes the need for counselling practitioners to have had wide-ranging life experiences. It encourages the selection of potential counselling practitioners from among those who have experience of more than one kind of job in their working life.

3.9   The potential benefits of counselling

The reason why counselling has assumed increasing importance as an active labour market measure over the past few years is because it has been recognised that information or training or work schemes on their own will not ensure the economic and social reintegration of those who are long-term unemployed. The importance of high quality "labour field counselling" is that it can assist other labour market measures to be targeted more accurately and thus avoid wastage of both financial and human resources. In other words one of the key benefits which counselling can bring is that of more cost effective usage of resources in the other active labour market measures.

More directly, counselling can bring benefits to those who use the services. For example it can quantify job placement successes, people who have accessed training and educational opportunities and numbers of people who have developed their own personal action plan. Counselling can serve as a catalyst for job opportunities and counsellors can act as brokers and advocates between potential employers and employees. What is less easy is to measure the indirect benefits of counselling such as the increase in self-confidence and motivation, and the development of life skills and the capacity to cope with change. If people are enabled to develop this capacity to handle change early on in their working lives it is likely that they will not need to make such intensive use of counselling services in the future and this will reduce the demand for resources for counselling in the longer term.

3.10 The attributes of "good" counselling

Eurocounsel has confirmed that there are a number of attributes of "good counselling" which are frequently listed in reports concerned with this subject. These include the following:

- being client centred;

- a process rather than a one-off solution;

- impartiality;

- confidentiality;

- inter-agency staff development and training;

- within a policy framework;

- quality assurance, including monitoring and evaluation.

In practice Eurocounsel has shown that many of these "good" attributes are not found and some, although setting an ideal, are in fact very difficult to fulfil in real situations. For example the aim to be client-centred is at the heart of much of what is considered to be good practice and yet it is one of the most difficult goals to achieve. In reality most organisations put their own objectives and the need to meet these first, and the needs of their clients second. We have already seen that for some practitioners this poses problems when they wish to offer more to their clients but the agency for which they work cannot allow the time or resources for this to happen. Striving towards a client centred approach should remain the goal but it is important to recognise that in reality there are many constraints.

The same kind of argument can be used with some of the other attributes of good practice. Eurocounsel has produced its own "Guide to Good Practice in Labour Market Counselling" [8] and one of the aims of this booklet is to set out both the ideal goals and also the realism which should be a part of these in any good practice. For example in relation to the problem of being client-centred described above it suggests that

> *"Practitioners should be able to demonstrate that they have a clear awareness of what forms of counselling they can offer, and at what level"*

This would allow the practitioner to be clear about their own boundaries in relation to what they can offer the client in their own situation so that they can make this clear to the client.

3.11 Conclusion

This chapter has described what forms counselling takes, methods used and some of the key issues in relation to counselling and guidance associated with helping individuals sort out their work related life. The next chapter turns to some more detailed and specific examples of issues which have been raised in the country by country research of the Eurocounsel programme.

4 HOW IS COUNSELLING DEVELOPING TO MEET THE NEEDS OF THE CHANGING LABOUR MARKET?

4.1 Introduction

Having described what counselling is and the different forms it takes in the last chapter, we turn now to examine how counselling services are developing in order to meet the needs of the changing labour market. This involves a consideration of the evolving role of counselling in different countries, and the part which employers, trade unions and users can and are playing in this evolution. We consider in depth what role counselling services are playing in relation to the changing nature of the labour market, and the various forms which work and activity take: part-time work; temporary and casual employment; social employment; work-sharing; are all part of this changing labour market. Finally we examine two key issues relating to the improvement of counselling services: the role of networking and linkages and the measurement and evaluation of counselling.

4.2 The evolving role of counselling services

The role of counselling has been evolving rapidly over the period of the Eurocounsel programme in most countries. In order to examine these changes in more depth it is useful to look at the background to counselling services which varies between different countries. For example, some countries have well developed and long established counselling services: in Denmark there is a long tradition of adult guidance and counselling stretching back to the beginning of this century. In other countries the provision of counselling has been developing and evolving but has been firmly rooted as an important aspect of that country's systems e.g. UK, Germany. In others, notably Italy but also to some extent Spain and Ireland, the importance of counselling is only just beginning to be realised and systems developed to meet the identified needs. It is interesting to note that in countries such as Ireland and Spain counselling is less well developed in the areas where subsistence agriculture has played an important part. In the more industrialised countries, where there was a clearer need to match the demand for labour with its supply, there was a direct need to develop services to assist in this matching process.

The changes to counselling provision over the period of the Eurocounsel programme relate mainly to the changing economic and labour market situation in most countries but the effect this has had has varied again from country to country and within countries. In Germany, where in the west of the country before reunification there was low unemployment and the counselling services regarded themselves as having to deal only with the most problematic of clients with specific difficulties in entering the labour market, there has been a radical change. Unemployment soared in the east after 1991 with the loss of over 3.5 million jobs. Resources were transferred from the west to the east to try to contain the situation. The reduction in resources in the west was then compounded by a recession in 1992 which led to the escalation of unemployment in the west too. The general effect of this upheaval on counselling service provision has been negative. Schumacher and Stiehr speak of the move "from counselling to control".[18] Although initially an important role was given to counselling services in the east of the country the pressure on resources has led to a reduction in service provision in both the east and the west with further reductions planned.

In other countries the growing pressure of unemployment, and the decline of the agricultural industry in particular, has led to a growth in counselling services as a possible route for individuals out of their unemployed situation. In Spain, the country with the highest unemployment in the EU in Spring 1994 (24.3%), the effects of the recession of the early 1990s are still being felt, despite an upturn since late 1993.[11] Government policy has changed to place more emphasis on the development of active labour market measures which has in turn led to increasing interest in the provision of counselling services. There is still concern however that the measures which are being introduced may increase the numbers of those who remain outside the provision of services: Gavira and Gonzalez believe that this is because active labour market measures tend to originate from and be designed for the north rather than the south of Europe. The role for counselling services is less clear in the south of Spain where there has been a long tradition of underemployment, seasonal work and casual work. Despite this there have been several developments in the provision of counselling initiated mainly by local bodies such as the Municipios and the Mancomunidades de Municipios (Association of Municipal Authorities).

Ireland has also started to develop more counselling services having recognised that there was in fact little by way of adult provision and specifically provision for the long-term unemployed. Many of the training programmes run or funded by FÁS now include counselling and guidance sessions and there is a new pilot National Guidance Service for Adults. The limited availability of placement services has also been highlighted and it is hoped that this will be addressed in the new Local Employment Services recommended by the Task Force on Long-term Unemployment and now being implemented by the Government. These will aim to co-ordinate services for the long-term unemployed on an area basis by co-ordinating action from all the agencies involved in supporting the long-term unemployed.[13]

Even in a country such as Denmark with its sophisticated structures for counselling *"there are signs that counselling in its traditional form seems to have some difficulties in responding to the labour market conditions of the 1990s".* [9] Efforts are being made to explore ways in which counselling can become more appropriate to present day needs: one of these is the increasing attention being given to ways to support self-help counselling initiatives led by the unemployed themselves. Counselling has an important role to play too in the activation measures which have been introduced by the Danish government.

In Italy the government's policy has tended to emphasise passive labour market measures and so it is not surprising that counselling services are not well developed. It is the only country in the Eurocounsel programme which still maintains an official public monopoly over employment services and this has been accompanied by *"a total absence of employment services, and in particular, counselling services"*.[19]

However it is clear that in the north of the country there are developments in counselling provision at regional and local levels. Although in theory the regions only have responsibility for careers guidance and vocational training in relation to the labour market, in practice some have gone further to develop their own laws and schemes in response to the need to fill gaps left by the state. This dichotomy of centralised versus decentralised provision leads to great variation in the level of services provided at local and regional levels. Under a regional law passed in Piedmont in 1991, CILO, (Centres of Local Employment Initiatives) have been established. These provide a co-ordinated approach to the provision of labour market services at local level and are new bodies resulting from a partnership between the Region and municipalities.

In the UK the main change which is apparent over the four year period of the Eurocounsel programme is the growing privatisation of counselling services. It is too early yet to assess the full impact which this change will have on service provision for the unemployed and the long-term unemployed but the fear is expressed that a two tier system will operate: those who can pay will go to private (and the assumption is made "of higher quality" services) while those who cannot afford to pay will be left with the core service provided by the Employment Service.[14]

The overall conclusion is that despite the reduction in service provision in Germany, which has been brought about by the rather unusual circumstances of that country, that the role of counselling in most countries is being increasingly recognised as an important one in the development of active labour market measures. (Even in Germany, although there are fewer counsellors compared to 1991, there is a sense that the need for such services is recognised more clearly now by decision makers than it was then). While in countries which have had a tradition of counselling such as Denmark and the UK, service provision is being adapted to meet the perceived needs of the labour market of the 1990s, in other countries such as Spain and Ireland it is being developed in recognition that it is an important active labour market measure.

4.3   The role of employers

The employers' representatives on the Advisory Committee for Eurocounsel have stressed their support for the programme throughout its four year period. This is indicative of the role which employers have to play as supporters for the provision of counselling services.

The most direct examples of employer involvement in counselling services come from situations of mass redundancy where the function of counselling is to prevent unemployment and long-term unemployment. The Arbeitsstiftung (Labour Foundations) in Austria and organisations such as British Coal Enterprise in the UK have involved the employer closely in the establishment of these preventive counselling services which work with those who are in danger of losing their job, or who have already done so, in industries which are facing major collapse. They are seen to be successful examples of the partnership approach to the provision of counselling services. [7]

If a closer link between economic and social policies is developed then it may become easier for employers to be further involved in supporting counselling services. The establishment of Businesses Against Social Exclusion (mentioned in chapter 2 of this report) is just one example of the ways in which employers can get involved. Some larger employers already provide counselling services for their employees who face redundancy; some have services which are available to employees about any subject at all which concerns them as they recognise that stress is a major factor in workplace absenteeism. Other roles which employers can play which support counselling provision is in providing work experience for the unemployed, being willing to consider applicants who are long-term unemployed who have been screened for a job by a counselling agency, and by being involved in helping to provide data for the analysis of local labour market conditions which remains one of the areas where counselling practitioners do not have enough information. One of the challenges for the future will be to find ways in which small and medium-sized businesses can become more fully involved in these ways too, in particular in providing counselling services for those facing redundancy and supporting existing employees to pursue training and learning opportunities.

4.4 The role of trade unions

The role of the trade unions with regard to counselling provision is still under-developed in many countries. In Ireland it is proposed that they should be one of the partners in the new Local Employment Services but it is not yet clear what that role should be. In Spain there is a sense that they are themselves providers of services whereas in Germany the role of the trade unions is seen to be not to seek solutions themselves but to prompt others to seek them. The situation in Denmark is different again due to the role which the trade unions play in that country in helping to administer the unemployment insurance funds. In Denmark too, trade unions, like employers, are represented on the coordinating structures for counselling services at regional level. In general, as with the employers the main direct role which trade unions have played is in helping to establish services in industries which are facing mass redundancies. They have proved important partners and catalysts for action in such instances in countries such as Austria, Germany and the UK.

The lack of clarity as to the role of the trade unions is unsurprising given that their traditional role is to support employees rather than those who do not have employment. Despite this it is important to recognise that there can be an important role for the trade unions in counselling provision. This may depend on some re-organisation of the traditional structures of the movement: for example encouraging more services for those who find themselves out of work may increase membership as there are now very few people who will not at some point of their working life face this situation. The unions may wish to consider the ways in which they can provide services directly themselves which would have the benefit of bringing them closer to their potential membership. As has been noted earlier the unions have already proposed a clear action plan with regard to their involvement in tackling social exclusion.[27] Other ways that trade unions can become more involved in counselling provision include the strengthening of links with counselling practitioners; the development of improved access to services through negotiation at national, regional and local levels; the provision of local labour market information and in supporting the right to information for users on opportunities and rights.

4.5 The role of users

The role which users can and should play has been one which has received increasing attention in Eurocounsel. Although there are few examples where users are actively involved in the initial design of services their views are regularly sought by many organisations as to what they think of the services they have experienced and how they would like to see them improved. The central idea of further involvement of users in the design of services is that this can be an empowering process in itself. There is also recognition that where users are involved in direct delivery of services, as in peer-counselling, that this can be both important for the individuals sharing counselling experience as well as an effective way to give assistance.

The role which users could play in the improvement of public services is also the subject of another research project of the European Foundation. The report "Public Welfare Services and Social Exclusion"[23] provides further detail on ways to improve user involvement in public services.

> *"The importance of involving consumers in the planning and delivery of public welfare services has now become more generally recognised."*

The specific means by which consumers can be more involved suggested in this report include increasing:

- access;
- choice;
- voice; and
- accountability.

The report also finds that decentralisation of services can assist in the process of allowing greater consumer involvement:

> *"..decentralisation increased consumer satisfaction with the convenience of services and frequently led to greater demand which could be satisfied more economically and efficiently."*

The issue of decentralisation versus centralisation in relation to counselling services is discussed more fully in the next chapter of this report.

4.6 The role of counselling linked to changes in the labour market

4.6.1 The search for new employment opportunities

The changing nature of the labour market and the importance of job creation at European level have been described in Chapter 2 of this report. Concern over unemployment is reflected in most countries in the European Union. Finding new job opportunities or creating and promoting them has become one of the main issues for many governments. Some examples of the approaches being taken in different countries are given below.

> In **Denmark** the policy of activation which focuses on ways to help more people become active in the labour market or in some form of work activity is the government's response to this situation. The job rotation scheme is the best known example of this policy. This allows employees to take sabbatical leave from their employment for a period of up to nine months and their place is filled by someone who has been long-term unemployed. The leave can be related to parenting, to a training or educational course or simply as a sabbatical.

> In **Germany** the main focus of current debate on labour market policy is on ways to find new employment opportunities. Amongst other initiatives a new Employment Protection Act was passed in August 1994 aimed at overcoming the barriers to taking

up employment and at creating subsidized new opportunities within the sphere of social employment measures. One interesting development contained within this Act is to extend the bridging allowance for those drawing unemployment benefit to make it easier for them to start up their own business. The search for new ways to create employment in Germany has included the following:

- trying out new models of working hours e.g. the Volkswagen model;
- looking to specific sectors for growth e.g. the environmental sector is seen as a growth area;
- new forms of social employment which it is hoped may lead to fully fledged market companies in the longer term e.g. in Western Germany the Social Companies and in Eastern Germany the ABSs (Work, Promotion, Employment and Structural Development Companies);
- self-employment (particularly seen to be important in east Germany).

Italy has a unique example of employment creation in the form of its Social Co-operatives which have been growing steadily in numbers. Other routes to employment creation are along the same lines as in other countries: self-employment; more part-time working etc.

Italy's Social Co-operatives

One of the most unique features of the non-profit-making sector in Italy is the social co-operatives. These have been gradually developed and there are now some 2,000 throughout Italy with 40,000 employees and thousands of volunteers. The social co-operatives are particularly aimed at the more marginalised in the labour market.

Article 1 of Law 381 (1991) provides the following definition:

"The purpose of social co-operatives is to pursue the general interest of the community in promoting the personal development and social integration of citizens by:

- *managing social, health and educational services;*
- *undertaking various activities, in agriculture, industry, commerce or services - whose aim is the occupational integration of disadvantaged individuals"*

It is the second of these functions, that of occupational integration, which relates most to the work of Eurocounsel. The social co-operatives combine entrepreneurship, and the need to create jobs, with the inclusion of the most disadvantaged who would not normally be considered, for reasons of productivity, in the traditional labour market.

In **Spain** the services sector is seen as the key area of growth generally although individual local areas are preparing various forms of economic strategies to take the best advantage of their local economic opportunities. In some instances (Badalona) this involves focusing on specialist services, in others (Andalusia) there has been growth in services which have low added value combined with inward investment by external companies.

In the **UK** there would appear to be less emphasis at government level on the search for new employment opportunities. In July 1994 the Employment Department was merged with the Education Department and the government Minister with responsibility for Education became the Minister for Education and Employment. While there can be seen to be some advantages to this merging of the two departments, particularly in allowing a greater streamlining of training policies, it is also true that it may reduce the focus of attention on employment and the need to find new ways to stimulate employment growth. This reflects the government's position in the UK that market forces should be allowed to run their own course without government intervention: that economic growth will in time trickle down to create jobs for all. Despite this, intervention both direct and indirect, does take place in the UK: for example, employers are given training and employment grants (TEGs) to induce them to employ unemployed people and employees who are on low pay are entitled to receive Family Credit, a top-up payment paid for through taxes.

4.6.2 The nature of changing opportunities for work and activity within the labour market

What are the opportunities for work and activity now being found in addition to full-time, "permanent" positions in the traditional primary labour market? To what extent are these being taken up by the unemployed and do practitioners see these as a way to labour market integration for their clients? The most commonly found "new opportunities" are self-employment and part-time work. Social employment, of varying kinds, is also important in most countries. The informal economy, although difficult to quantify, remains an important source of activity and additional income for many unemployed people. Some further comments about some of the Eurocounsel findings on these changes in the labour market are given below.

Self employment

Self-employment appears to be the most common opportunity for work creation not associated directly with the traditional opportunities on the primary labour market. There appear to be different perceptions on the part of counselling practitioners as to how suitable a route this is for many unemployed people: the UK research found that *"some of the agencies interviewed were perhaps a little too ready to judge that self-employment was not an option for their 'type of client'"* [14] while in Spain the research showed that self-employment and establishing small enterprises were seen to be the main "alternative routes to employment" by users of the services themselves and the main area in which any professional counselling linked to new ways to work was found.

In most countries the advice and counselling available to those who wish to set up their own business is undertaken by organisations separate from those which undertake other forms of employment counselling and adult guidance. This is not always helpful, particularly where linkages between the different agencies involved are weak (see later in this chapter under "Linkages").

Social employment

Social employment covers both the community work programmes established by many governments (e.g. Community Employment in Ireland; community work contracts in Spain etc) and the independent social enterprises which have been successful in some countries, for example the Social Co-operatives in Italy and the insertion enterprises in France. The need for social employment of varying kinds is increasingly recognised as a means by which those who have been long-term unemployed can begin to return to the labour market. This area of opportunities is sometimes referred to as the Intermediate Labour Market.[35]

Voluntary work

Griffiths[22] quotes from research undertaken by the Employment Service in the UK on Volunteering and Unemployment in 1994.

"Only a small proportion of unemployed people considered doing voluntary work to occupy their time, a much higher proportion were involved in other kinds of leisure activities. Furthermore, those who were participating in some type of voluntary work, were doing so for only a small amount of their time (the majority for less than five hours per week). Therefore few unemployed volunteers were treating voluntary work as the equivalent of a full time job."

("Volunteering and Unemployment - a Literature Review" Employment Service REB92 February 1994)

The above quote, perhaps surprising given the image of the UK as a country where voluntary work is fairly embedded, reflects the findings in other countries too. In Germany it was apparent that unemployed people would not even consider voluntary work unless there was some form of payment. However there are of course instances where the opposite is found: in Badalona, Spain, municipal-authority practitioners pointed out that "there are people who want to work even if they are not paid" and because there are so many in this position the municipal authority is considering establishing unpaid work-experience schemes, as a first temporary step into a job.

Informal economy

Although the informal economy is not an area in which counselling practitioners specialise for obvious reasons, it is nevertheless an important part of the means of survival for unemployed people, not only in terms of the income it can provide but also in allowing people to remain active and their self-image to remain positive. Plant[9] points out that in Denmark people *in* employment seem to be more active in the informal economy than those who are unemployed as they tend to have better contacts and access to tools which they can use for work outside their own job. So the temptation to see the informal economy as the prerequisite of the unemployed only should be avoided.

Gavira and Gonzalez [21] state that the "submerged economy" in Spain has been a traditional part of life in rural areas where people were not used to full-time jobs in the primary labour market. They note that there is increasing competition even within this informal sector because of the pressures in the primary labour market, particularly due to the reduction in jobs for unskilled and low skilled workers. There is some evidence (from the UK and Germany) that counsellors can play a role in helping those who have built up a business or self-employment on the informal market to transfer into the formal labour market and become "legitimate".

4.6.3 Counselling practice in relation to the changing opportunities for work and activity

In the UK there is evidence from the research undertaken that apart from professionally qualified careers guidance staff, counselling practitioners are not trained to and do not see themselves as being responsible for providing counselling across the whole range of potential opportunities open to an individual. Their scope of knowledge tends to be confined to the area of the aims and objectives of their own organisation. They would regard it as their responsibility to have sufficient general knowledge to be able to refer clients to appropriate counselling agencies for advice which they could not offer themselves e.g. on self-employment if they were a training provider.[14]

In **Denmark** the research shows that counsellors are aware of increasing flexibility in the labour market and the increase in part-time work for example but do not see it as their role to advocate such options. Much of the counselling in Denmark which is linked to these alternative opportunities for work and activity is linked closely to the job rotation and adult education schemes which have been formalised as an alternative to jobs in the primary labour market. It is pointed out that as most of the counsellors are based in educational institutions and are wage earners as opposed to entrepreneurs and risk-takers that it may be alien for them to feel comfortable advising their clients about alternative higher risk options. They need more training in this area if they are to be effective.[9]

In **Italy** the research indicates that only a small part of counsellors' work focuses on these alternative opportunities for work and activity. Part of the reason for this is thought to be their lack of understanding of the changes affecting the world of work:

> *"...counsellors must be able to understand the changes that are affecting the economic and social system so they can make their clients aware of the changing nature of the labour market."* [12]

In **Spain** the role of counsellors in relation to alternative opportunities appears to revolve primarily around assisting those who wish to consider self-employment. The forms which this provision takes are threefold:

- information provision to help people solve the practical problems of setting themselves up as self-employed;

- information and training on enterprise management techniques, although this tends to be restricted in terms of access to unemployed business and economic graduates or owners of small enterprises rather than to people who are just unemployed;

- counselling as part of an agenda setting exercise which takes place over a period of time; there are different examples of this kind of agenda setting depending on which target group it is aimed at and on who is providing it. Examples include the Taller de Emprendedores (Entrepreneurs Workshop); the Emprendedores programme for women entrepreneurs (funded by the European NOW programme) and special supported integration programmes for people with mental and physical difficulties.

Gavira and Gonzalez[11] identify two main types of practitioner: those who work from a structural perspective which is characterised by their ability to make the connections between theoretical knowledge and real life and to strike a balance between the aims of their organisation and the needs expressed by users of the services; and those who work from positive analytical perceptions of the local situation, who tend to separate theory and life and the objectives of their organisation and the users.[11]

The importance of local labour market information

There is evidence from several countries that the level of knowledge of counsellors regarding their local labour market is not high. The research points to the general need for greater understanding of the world of work.

"The lack of employee insight into national economic and business correlations is not an exception but, rather, the rule and one that applies fairly equally to both eastern and western German counselling organisations." [10]

Understanding future labour market trends is also an area which is lacking:

"Counselling practitioners acknowledge that when it comes to defining the industries of the future, there is no concrete information on the situation, which means that practitioners take their direction, on a day to day basis, from their own experience." [11]

The need for adjustments to tax and welfare systems to complement counselling provision for the long-term unemployed

Ronayne, Murphy and Corrigan[13] point out that, despite the insecurity associated with some of these alternative opportunities, this "atypical" employment does offer an opportunity for the unemployed to re-enter the labour market. However they stress the fact that for many long-term unemployed people this opportunity will not make sense unless there are adjustments to the tax and welfare system so that it becomes worthwhile to take up part-time or short-term contract work. The Irish Government has introduced two important measures to attempt to tackle this issue which are described in the box below.

The Back to Work Allowance Scheme allows the unemployed to take up paid employment or become self-employed while retaining 75% of their social welfare payments in the first year and 50% in the second. In addition all secondary benefits are retained. The scheme allows participants who have been long-term unemployed to test out employment options and to retain some financial security as they re-enter the labour market. The scheme is administered by the Department of Social Welfare. At the end of October 1994 the number of people participating in the scheme was 4,020 of which 2,691 were self-employed. The scheme will only consider those who are entering self-employment or full-time employment. It is administered by Job Facilitators who operate on a regional basis and act as mediators between the unemployed and employers.

> **The Area Allowance Enterprise Scheme** (AAES) is administered by the Area Based Partnership Companies (ABPCs). The scheme is targeted on the long-term unemployed and provides support for those who wish to establish an enterprise or become self-employed. Under the scheme the participants retain 100 per cent of their social welfare payments and all secondary payments for the period of one year while engaged in enterprise activities. At the end of 1993 there were 740 participants on this scheme.

The Area Enterprise Allowance Scheme is similar to other financial support schemes to help the unemployed establish a business found in other countries. (e.g. Denmark; UK; Germany). The Irish Community Employment programme allows the unemployed who take up part-time or temporary contract work to continue to receive benefit which is an important recognition of the incentives which may be needed to encourage the long-term unemployed to take up such routes back into work.

The role of counsellors in relation to the changing opportunities on the labour market

In some countries counsellors see themselves as catalysts for these alternative opportunities. For example, in eastern Germany the way in which this happens is described as being

> *"..by acting as an interface between those seeking advice and the various players on the labour market"*

such as in the case of the Counselling Centre for Women wishing to Return to Work.[10] In the west it was the view of the representative of the social welfare organisation "Diakonisches Werk an Der Saar" that the entire secondary labour market had emerged and been structured through the ideas of the counselling services.

However, others have raised the question as to whether there is a moral dilemma for counselling practitioners in advising clients to pursue opportunities which they know may well be insecure, low paid and temporary. On balance it is felt that the counselling practitioners have a duty to enable their clients to make their own decisions having provided them with full information so that they understand the pros and cons of any option they may pursue.

One of the dangers of the emerging opportunities for work, in particular those associated with the secondary labour market and with short-term jobs, is that they will not help to break the cycle of unemployment, short term work, and return to unemployment, which is the norm for so many unemployed and underemployed people. Hurley[14] highlights the need for counselling practitioners to assist clients to make vertical progression in their search for a path back into the labour market. Too often the progression is horizontal and the client remains in the unemployment trap going round in a circle which alternates between training in job search followed by gaining a short term job, followed by unemployment, followed by another short-term job and so on.

"There is a need to ensure that progression is vertical, into good quality opportunities where individuals are improving on their skills and learning in order that they can progress up the skills and wages ladder" [14]

The role of EU funding

There is increasing recognition of the importance of European funding both in supporting the creation of new ways to work and in supporting the counselling which is provided as an integral part of this. One example of this is given in the box below.

European Funding Creating Jobs

In Storstroms Amt (Denmark) resources from the EU Social Fund helped to create the innovative Medieval Museum project in which a production school joined forces with professionals from the local museum in Nykobing Falster, and voluntary workers, in creating a unique blend of a living museum and an activation project.[9]

The NOW, HORIZON, INTERREG, KONVER, RECHAR and RENAVAL programmes in addition to the ERDF and ESF funds have all been cited during Eurocounsel as having assisted in the creation of new employment opportunities. Given that counselling is often a component part of such programmes it can be seen that European funding is playing an important role. It is also involved directly in the funding of service provision through the initiatives mentioned in Chapter 2.6.2.

4.6.4 Conclusion

Although the importance of the alternative opportunities for work and activity is recognised and there is evidence that in relation to self-employment counselling is available, the research undertaken into this topic indicates that there is very little counselling specifically geared towards helping the long-term unemployed consider these alternative routes to work. The reasons for this appear to be lack of knowledge on such options on the part of counsellors themselves and because the majority of counselling practitioners across the participating countries are working in the public employment service sector which is already under enormous pressure to meet the basic information needs of its clients.

In Denmark the reason for this absence of counselling was explained as being due to the fact that most counselling practitioners there see themselves as educationalists and social workers and less as *"promoters of entrepreneurship"* or risk-taking.[9]

Some of the country reports (e.g. Denmark and Spain) raised the issue that even where counselling does exist (whether it be in relation to matching supply and demand on the primary labour market or in relation to these alternative opportunities for work and activity) that there is danger that some groups will be marginalised: the Spanish report highlights the fact that as new counselling bodies emerge (due to the pressure on the public employment services) their success is measured by how many users they place into jobs and therefore they concentrate their energies on those who are more employable. Gavira and Gonzalez[11] suggest that those most at risk of exclusion from counselling services in Spain are unemployed people with low or very low levels of education and, somewhat surprisingly, university graduates who for various reasons tend not to make use of the services available.[11]

4.7 Linkages

An important issue for the development and improvement of counselling services is that of the linkages between the different providers of counselling services and between such services and other organisations involved in the labour market. Throughout Eurocounsel there has been recognition that networks are an important element in the effectiveness of counselling provision.[1 & 2] The complexity of service provision and its apparent ever-widening diversity make such linkages even more important. Without linkages between the different service providers there may be duplication of effort, a wastage of scarce resources and a lack of transparency in terms of the user knowing which agency to approach. Agencies themselves may not be in a position to know what other providers are able to offer.

There are many different kinds of linkages. There are those between counselling providers themselves, from labour market, educational or business development backgrounds. Such linkages may be formalised or may be informal and can take place at local, regional and national levels. Then there are the linkages between counselling providers and those involved in other ways in the development of the labour market and services for the unemployed, such as employers, trade unions and those with responsibility for local economic development planning. There are linkages which remain within the public sector and those which cut across the public, private and non-government/voluntary sectors.

The main questions which we sought to answer in the Eurocounsel research were as follows:

- what linkages already exist?
- who is involved in the networking?
- what problems are there and how could they be solved?
- why are linkages important to the work of counselling services?

The European Commission's report "Educational and Vocational Guidance in the European Community"[33] provided a useful starting point for analysing the different kinds of linkages which occur and has been used as the basis for the research in Eurocounsel. The framework suggests that linkages between service providers take place at different levels:

- ***Communication*** where no working patterns are changed, but efforts are made to help services understand what each other has to offer so that they can cross-refer clients appropriately and avoid overlap;

- *Co-operation* where two or more services co-operate on a specific joint task;

- *Co-ordination* where two or more services alter their working patterns to bring them more closely into line with one another, while remaining within their existing professional boundaries;

- *Cross-fertilisation* where efforts are made to encourage services to share and exchange skills and in effect to work across professional boundaries in ways that are likely to re-draw the boundaries themselves;

- *Integration* where the process is developed to the point where the boundaries between services disappear altogether.

In addition to an analysis based on the above framework, the research examined the kinds of links which exist between organisations not involved directly in counselling, such as employers and trade unions, and counselling providers. It then looked at the barriers which can exist to the creation and sustainability of linkages and at the benefits which they can bring. Finally some conclusions were drawn as to how linkages can be improved in the future.

It should be noted at the outset that one country, Denmark, has highly developed linkages in terms of its counselling provision and so many examples are drawn from this source. Other countries are at various stages of developing such linkages but none of the remaining five countries has the same degree of formalisation and sophistication of linkages as found in Denmark.

4.7.1 What is the rationale for formal linkages?

There are several reasons why policy makers or counselling agencies wish to establish formal linkages. These include the following:

- the need to secure financial and technical resources;

- the need to avoid the duplication of services and to reduce costs; (although this runs alongside the general view that diversity of service provision is helpful to users, despite the complexity, as it allows for greater choice);

- the need to improve the situation of groups of unemployed people by applying political pressure; linkages can facilitate counselling agencies to advocate policy changes;

- the facilitation of the integration into the labour market of the groups which may be most difficult to place by collaboration between a range of services, and by direct contact with employers.

4.7.2 Analysis according to the framework

With the exception of Denmark, where all five types of linkages are found, most countries have several examples of linkages which involve communication and co-operation, but less frequently co-ordination, and rarely of cross-fertilisation or integration. The latter is even seen not to be desirable by agencies in the UK and Germany for example, where the high level of competition between different providers for clients and resources is not conducive to a further blurring of the boundaries between them In Denmark however there are several examples of cross-fertilisation. These include cross-sector appointments as well as the establishment of joint structures where counselling and guidance professionals work together. One such example, Knudepunktet (the Knot), is described in the box below. This example provides, from the client's point of view, an *integrated* service.

THE KNOT

The Knot is situated in the small provincial town of Frederiksvaerk in Frederiksborg County. The municipal counselling and employment staff have joined forces with the local employment office staff to work closely on the same premises with each other's clients. The services offered include an open self-service information centre on training options and job vacancies; individual vocational and educational counselling offered by the staff from the different organisations involved.[9]

4.7.3 Formal versus informal links

Gavira and Gonzalez[11] state that although policy makers tend to claim that there is co-operation and co-ordination, those working at local level tend to perceive that there is no time for these and that most linkages are in fact informal in nature. This is particularly true of rural areas where there are fewer organisations involved and people working in them have the opportunity to know their counterparts.

"In general, the links that are established have more to do with goodwill and personal affinities between practitioners than with policies that encourage links to improve efficiency. In many cases, these links are more effective than those established formally between services, since they serve to increase the transparency of local counselling services. Similarly, it is often informal links that facilitate users' access to services."[11]

All the countries involved in this research have highlighted the existence of these informal linkages and their importance: the advantages of these are seen to be that they are readily developed and can involve close working relationships at local level; the disadvantages are that they rely on personal relationships which can change when the personnel change and which do not allow good practice to be easily translated to other areas or to policy formulation.

4.7.4 Co-ordination issues

In **Italy**, Maiello and Geroldi point out that there is a need for a co-ordination unit at local level *"to serve as the political and professional point of reference and to perform the role of integrating the various agents that may usefully contribute their resources and specialised skills..."*.[12] In **Ireland** this form of co-ordinating body is to be found in the Area Based Partnership Companies (ABPCs) which operate at a local level and which *"provide a structure that can facilitate the integrated or co-ordinated development of labour market services within discrete geographical areas."*[13] The ABPCs help to establish formal links between the providers of labour market and other services in the localities in which they operate, although it is noted that they have had varying success in this. The Local Employment Services which are currently being established are likely to play a similar co-ordinating role for services for the long-term unemployed.

In the **UK** there was no evidence in the local area researched (Inverclyde) of linkages with services being co-ordinated by one organisation on behalf of others nor was there any desire for joint co-ordination or integration of services. There were a number of informal educational and training networks but no evidence of any strategic level moves towards co-ordination or integration. However it is recognised that this will vary from area to area.

In **Spain** an important example of co-ordination is that between some of the municipal authorities which have established Mancomunidades. One of these is the service established by the Mancomunidad del Bajo Guadalquivir described in the box below.

> **The Mancomunidad del Bajo Guadalquivir**
>
> The Mancomunidad del Bajo Guadalquivir provides an example of setting up and developing an integrated model of employment counselling services which is adapted to the local socio-economic circumstances. It has developed formal collaborative links with funding and reciprocal guarantee bodies such as the Federacion de Pequenos y Medianos Empresarios (Federation of Small and Medium Sized Businesses) and the Organizacion de Agricultores y Ganaderos (Farmers' Organisation) and the provincial Council with a view to running training activities. It has also developed service integration links with INEM so that it can operate a full counselling process for unemployed people and enterprises and also promote local enterprises.[11]

4.7.5 Linkages with employers

Most countries recognise the importance of establishing good relations between counselling services and employers but there is evidence that these could be greatly improved. In Germany, Schumacher and Stiehr have traced the relationship with employers over the period of the Eurocounsel programme and note how this has changed in western Germany: at the early stages of the programme the perception among both counsellors and employers of the long-term unemployed was that they were people with distinct personal problems who would have difficulty fitting into the labour market. Employers even considered that because the long-term unemployed had been through intensive educational and social programmes that they had been cushioned against the tough requirements of the labour market and this made them unemployable. Employers therefore saw little point in establishing relations with counselling services. However as the labour market changed and more people faced unemployment the attitude of both employers and counselling organisations has begun to change. Eleven of the twelve counselling organisations interviewed have established linkages with employers and their organisations although the degree of success remains varied. The movement towards greater collaboration with employers may be speeded up as more counselling organisations consider the possibility, now available to them for the first time, of applying for a licence as a private employment agency.[10]

Hurley[14] notes that many of the counselling agencies in the area researched in the UK approach employers to participate in a variety of opportunities being offered to people looking for work. Employers may be asked to provide work experience placements, to take part in a college careers event, or carry out mock interviews with unemployed people. It is a relationship which is sought out and seen to be influential.

4.7.6 Linkages with trade unions

Links with trade unions are less commonly found than with employers. In the **UK** the reason given for this is that the area involved in the research has many high technology companies which are non-unionised. Another reason given is that the structure of the Local Enterprise Company network in Scotland and the Training and Enterprise Councils in England is employer led with no automatic right of representation for trade unions. This makes it extremely difficult for trade unions to be considered as partners at this strategic area level.[14]

In **Germany** too there is less contact between the counselling agencies surveyed and trade unions than there is with employers. What contact there is tends to take place at the political level rather than in the provision of practical support or co-operation with the counselling agencies. The perception of a lack of constructive contact is shared both by the counselling agencies and by the trade unions interviewed.[10]

The situation in **Denmark** with regard to trade union involvement is different due to the role which trade unions play in administering the unemployment insurance funds. This leads to closer contacts with counselling agencies. For example the local public employment offices, AF, co-operate directly with the unemployment insurance fund offices concerning, for instance, the personal action plans of each unemployed member of the insurance funds. All the personal plans must be approved by the AF and sent on to the unemployment insurance fund offices for further processing before any funding is dispensed to the unemployed person. As the Danish report points out, "*This calls for mutual referral and understanding, and flexible co-operation between the two systems.*"[9] It is noted that this somewhat complex system may be improved with the introduction of computer programmes for administrative purposes.

4.7.7 Links across sectors

In general it appears that there are few links across sectors. For example in **Spain** the research highlights the lack of links between education and work despite legal provisions at national level concerning co-ordination and co-operation. The links in Spain between those involved in social welfare and those in work related counselling are also weak although there is an exception to this in the Instituto de la Mujer (Women's Institute). In general there are few links between agencies in the public and private sectors, although the exception is the private centres which work in collaboration with the Autonomous Administrations as their continuing presence within the network and the funding it implies depend on the degree of occupational integration they achieve for their clients.[11]

In the **UK** the lack of linkages between the self-employment/small business counselling agencies and those involved in counselling for employment and training is noted. The two sides tend to be separate although some referrals are made between them. It is suggested that this is an area in which a more strategic approach to linkages is needed so that unemployed people can benefit more readily from all that the combined services have to offer them. The same separation between the socially and educationally focused counselling services in educational, training and labour market institutions on the one hand and those concerned with business development on the other is noted in the Danish situation. This separation relates back to the need, established in EU policy documents, for social policy to be an integral part of economic policy, which in turn necessitates better links at local level between social development measures and local economic development. Counselling services could help to build these links and act as the bridge between the different sectors.

4.7.8 Barriers to linkages

There are a number of different barriers to the establishment and maintenance of linkages identified in the Eurocounsel research.

Lack of strategic co-ordination

Several reports highlight the lack of strategic co-ordination at central policy making level or at regional level which it is thought could facilitate the formation of linkages. In **Ireland** it is noted that even the core labour market services appear to have little strategic co-ordination despite the number of government departments which are involved in some way in their provision. There is little attempt either to provide formal structures and opportunities for communication and co-operation between implementing bodies and the personnel working in these. One of the consequences of this is that there is a lack of comprehensive documentation regarding the labour market services and programmes available for the unemployed.[13]

In the **UK** this lack of strategic co-ordination at policy making level is also noted as a barrier to the effective development of linkages between counselling services. No one agency in the area researched has agreed the responsibility for ensuring that progression between services occurs although this "seamless process for guidance" was identified as one of the purposes of having linkages.

"There is no joint strategic framework in place which can address some of the fundamental gaps in provision and dovetail with a strategy on developing both the skills base of the population and the local economy whether through training, employment, or small business development. The lack of a joint strategic framework may be at least partly the result of the lack of linkage at policy level by those who have responsibility for taking decisions on funding, policy direction, and management."[14]

The presence of a strategic framework is best illustrated by examining the Danish model which as stated at the start of this section is the most developed in terms of linkages. The box below describes this model.

> **The Danish model of service co-ordination**
>
> Co-ordination is maintained between all professional counselling services in Denmark by the same legislation, the Educational and Vocational Act of 1981 which established the National Council of Educational and Vocational Guidance (R.U.E.) with a wide representation including national education and employment authorities, women's organisations, the social partners, and counsellors. In 1994 new guidelines were issued whereby regional careers guidance and counselling committees, known as VFU (Vejledningsfaglige Udvalg) were re-established in the 14 counties along with local committees in a number of the 275 municipalities. The VFU are sub-committees of the regional labour market councils (Regionale Arbejdsmarkedsrad, RAR) on which are represented the social partners, the municipalities in the region, the county and regional educational institutions.[9]

The Spanish example quoted earlier of the Mancomunidades del Bajo Guadalquivir is an illustration too of the kind of co-ordination which can assist in helping linkages to work effectively, which will be further facilitated if the process is transparent and externally evaluated.

Despite the formal procedures for co-ordination in the Danish situation described in the box above, it is still apparent that there is sometimes a lack of genuine co-ordination and common approaches to avoid overlap and the waste of counselling resources. As Plant[9] states:

"To meet such criticism, a number of counselling centres and 'shops' have been established in order to pool the expertise of counsellors from different sectors within a common framework. Via such mechanisms the differences in the sectorally based expert knowledge are maintained, and, simultaneously, local co-ordination of counselling efforts can take place. The focus in recent years has, precisely, been on establishing such joint multi-disciplinary bases of counselling."

Competition

Another barrier to linkages which has been much referred to by the various country researchers is that of competition which is if anything increasing rather than decreasing with the removal of the monopoly of public employment services in countries such as Spain and Germany. In addition to the direct competition for clients and for resources there is the problem of *"different political stances of organisations and individuals which give rise to rivalries that make collaboration difficult."*[11] sometimes these differences in principles relate directly to the provision of counselling: for example, in Germany, independent services which apply the principle of the voluntary nature of accepting counselling and support services find it difficult to have close relations with the social welfare offices which use compulsive means to make people attend by threatening the withdrawal of benefits for non-attendance on schemes.[10]

The problem of competition appears to be more easily dealt with where the different agencies involved have clearly defined functions i.e. where they can see they are not in direct competition with each other.

Lack of equality

Another barrier which has been highlighted is that of the lack of equality between those involved in the networking relationship. This tends to happen where one of the partners involved has the power to fund the others. In such linkages the element of compulsion and of rivalry between those seeking to gain funding can damage a real sense of co-operation.

Other barriers to effective linkages include dependency on informal and personal relationships which have been mentioned above (although it is also recognised that such informal relationships often produce very effective linkages while the people involved remain in post) and the fact that different organisations may have very different cultures and objectives.

4.7.9 *The benefits of linkages*

Linkages can bring many benefits, both to the users of the services and also to those who work in them. They can also be seen to be helpful to policy makers who can learn more easily from the experience of a range of counselling providers where these are grouped together and able to distil their experience.

Benefits for users

The most important benefit for users is that the linking of the wide range of counselling services which is available in most countries can help to make what is on offer more transparent. It becomes easier to access the services and to be referred from one to another where this is appropriate. Improved access to services should in turn mean that the user has greater likelihood of a successful outcome in terms of finding an appropriate path to suit their own situation.

Benefits for counselling practitioners

One of the benefits noted in the German report, which relates back to the discussion on competition above, is that linkages provide an opportunity to "observe the enemy"! In less competitive circumstances, linkages assist the transfer of good practice between practitioners. Other benefits include the gaining of funding and also the opportunity it can present for exchange of ideas and methods. In some of the Danish examples, where cross-fertilisation and integration are being achieved, the opportunity to work in a multi-disciplinary team and to train together clearly brings advantages to the practitioners in terms of their own professional development and mutual support as well as improving service to the users.

Benefits for policy makers

The most important benefits which formal linkages bring is the opportunity for policy makers to learn from on-the-ground experience of counselling practitioners to inform their own deliberations with regard to the development of active labour market measures. Improved linkages and coordination of services can strengthen strategic planning of service delivery and provide a clearer identification of the different roles each organisation is to play in the overall plan.

4.7.10 Conclusions

The need for linkages could be seen to be merely a reflection of the disjointed and unco-ordinated system of service provision which has been allowed to develop in most countries. The number of counselling providers has mushroomed and as each new need is identified so too a new agency or service is created to meet the need. Provision has not grown out of a centrally planned policy but instead has been reactive in its development: linkages are needed to make sense of this diverse and poorly co-ordinated system.

The formal linkages appear to be those which have been established from the top-down. In many countries, with the exception of Denmark, these formal linkages are scarce or exist in name only, the real linkages taking place at the informal level. There are some examples of local co-ordination which cut across different sectors but these are rare although the need for such strategic co-ordination is recognised in at least some of the countries.

One of the main barriers to effective linkages is perceived to be the growing competition between service providers although it is interesting to note that in Denmark, where there is a wide range of service providers, the multi-disciplinary approach is one which appears to be finding favour at present. If there is to be real co-ordination, rather than just a patching up of poorly linked services, the Danish report suggests that counselling services which wish to co-operate should be designed from the outset to take part in a co-ordinated effort.

In terms of the social partners it is seen that the relevance of linkages with employers is understood although there is much that could be done to improve relations in this area. However with regard to the trade unions there is less sense of what purpose such linkages could provide: there is a need for a thorough re-examination of the role which trade unions could play in relation to the provision of counselling services for the unemployed.

The need to develop linkages across sectors, the social, educational, labour market, and business development areas in particular, will assist in the development of a more holistic approach to the provision of counselling services and to more coherent local labour market development. There are still clear divides in all countries between at least some of these sectors. A project is currently being undertaken by CEDEFOP concerned with the integration of the full range of counselling, guidance training and labour market insertion measures for young people at local levels.

4.8 The measurement of the quality and effectiveness of counselling

Another important issue for the development and improvement of counselling provision is the question of how to measure and evaluate the quality and effectiveness of counselling services and to feed back results into the planning of counselling services as an integral element of an active labour market policy. As part of the Eurocounsel research a literature review was undertaken in each of the participating countries so that an assessment could be made as to what existed in relation to this subject in each country. This initial step was followed by analysis of practice at local level. The key questions which were addressed were:

- who has an interest in having counselling services evaluated and why?
- who undertakes the evaluation
- what methods are applied?
- what features and effects are measured?
- is any use made of the results and by whom?
- what problems can be recognised?
- how can the situation be improved?

There are clear differences between the different countries in relation to this topic which might be expected given what has been said about the varying levels of the development of counselling services in general. In two countries, the **UK** and **Denmark**, there is a fairly long tradition of measurement or assessment of some description; in others there is a growing recognition of the importance to develop an "assessment culture" (e.g. **Spain**) if only to meet the requirements of European funding criteria. In others the development of a methodology for evaluation in relation to labour market services is still in its infancy (**Germany, Ireland**). In several of the countries where evaluation of counselling services does exist it is undertaken as part of broader labour market measures and programmes rather than independently (**Italy, Germany, Ireland**).

A separate bibliography has been compiled which draws together the literature review on evaluation from the six participating countries.

4.8.1 The rationale for evaluation

The provision of counselling connected to "finding a path" related to work, has been shown in Chapter 3 of this report to be highly complex. It includes a whole range of different types of intervention. It has also been seen that counselling of this nature crosses the economic, social and educational sectors in relation to policy development. It is therefore likely to be an area which is not easy to evaluate as there are a huge number of different approaches and actors which could be involved as well as varying functions which are being fulfilled.

As unemployment in Europe has risen, the need to measure the impact of different labour market policies has become more pressing. Within labour market measures the case for counselling still has to be made in some quarters although there have been some claims made already as to its cost effectiveness. For example one of the findings in the ERGO programme's Phase 1 report was that counselling was most cost-effective in terms of costs per additional job entry.[31] One of the reasons why evaluations are undertaken in some countries is to assess the cost-benefits of counselling and to evaluate the outcomes in terms of outputs against inputs.

> **The Economic Value of Guidance**
>
> Killeen, White and Watts publication "The Economic Value of Counselling" published in the UK was an initial attempt to explore the ways in which the economic value can be measured. They made a rough estimate that, every one per cent of occupational mismatch could be worth £10 million to the Exchequer (based on the assumption that occupational mismatch accounts for 10% of unemployment). The argument is that effective counselling and guidance can save the Exchequer money by helping to match the supply and demand side of the labour market more accurately.[48]

The reasons why it is important to measure and evaluate counselling provision is not just connected to assessing its cost effectiveness. Other reasons include the following:

- *the need to quantify its achievements;* This is important because counselling may have effects on the labour market which do not benefit everyone. It may make some people stronger on the labour market at the expense of others. For example if the long-term unemployed are given intensive counselling which helps them to secure a job then this may at the same time displace someone who has been out of work for only a short time and who has not received counselling.

- *the need to measure the quality of what is offered* particularly as there is a growth in countries, such as the UK, in the market of services and as users need to know what the difference in terms of quality is between the different services they are being offered;

- *the need for accountability* as most counselling is publicly funded;

- *to assess its technical implementation rather than its success or outcomes*; this involves monitoring the process of what is taking place rather than focusing on its outcomes;

- *to identify gaps in provision* so that these can be rectified. An example of this is given in the box below.

> **Identifying gaps in provision**
>
> In Denmark an evaluation of the scheme to provide the long-term unemployed with a grant to help them establish their own business was undertaken. Concerning counselling, the grant holders were asked whether they had received enough advice and counselling from the AF office (who administer the grant) about the enterprise grant scheme before they started. 34% said yes and 31% said they had received none. The corresponding figures concerning the counselling given in A-Kasser (the unemployment insurance funds) revealed that two-thirds had received counselling on this particular topic i.e. one third had received none. One of the problems in both these institutions seemed to be that counselling staff had little or no experience in relation to private enterprise development.[9]

As Maiello and Geroldi[12] point out, since counselling is a process it is actually possible for it to be constantly improved. The process as well as the outcomes should be evaluated.

4.8.2 Who is interested in having counselling services evaluated?

As might be expected the public employment services in most countries tend to be interested in having counselling services evaluated although this is not as widespread as might be expected. INEM, the **Spanish** public employment service responsible for managing central government's employment policies takes only internal quantitative assessments of its counselling services although there is beginning to be a push for further work in this direction.[11] There are examples of local offices undertaking assessment of specific training and counselling programmes. In **Germany** it appears that there is some work being undertaken as to the success of employment counselling in the State employment offices but the results of this work are only available internally and not to the wider public. In the **UK** however there have been a number of studies undertaken by the former Employment Department which has for a number of years been interested in assessing its policy and practice in offering employment guidance to unemployed people. The effects of initiatives such as Restart Courses, Job Review Workshops and Job Clubs have all been measured examining their different effects and outcomes.[14]

Individual projects can also be interested in having an evaluation of their work undertaken. In **Italy** where counselling services are fairly new, it is noted that there is a positive desire on the part of agencies such as the CILOs to have their work assessed. This is one way in which they can have their work legitimized:

"People who feel their work is new and unique want it to be acknowledged and recognised. In general, though, the kind of evaluation that practitioners particularly want is qualitative: what impact has my work had on the people who received counselling?"[12]

Another reason why individual projects and organisations may be interested in evaluation is that it may help them to make the case for further funding.

One funding body which has certainly stimulated more action on assessment and evaluation in countries where this was not already a tradition is the European Union. The regulations for the Structural Funds state the following:

"it is vital to have the necessary elements to assess the socio-economic impact of Community intervention. Assessment processes must be based on the principles of co-operation and transparency that are common to all aspects of the reform"(quoted in 11)

In Spain this appears to have had great influence on stimulating action in projects which are co-funded and in generating an interest in the development of an "assessment culture".

4.8.3 Who undertakes evaluations?

Government departments, and in Spain, Autonomous Governments, can undertake their own evaluations. Frequently however they employ or sub-contract such work to independent research institutes and consultants. A number of academic studies are undertaken by universities for their own sake and some of the more innovative work in some countries, for example Spain, has been undertaken through this source. In Italy it is noted that problems can be encountered when someone whose role it is to support a project is also given the task of evaluating it: clearly in such instances it is difficult to be completely objective. Generally there will be more value in having an objective and independent evaluation undertaken.

4.8.4 Methods used

The methods used in the different countries have similarities as well as differences. Both quantitative and qualitative methods are used although the emphasis has tended to be on the former.

A number of ways to measure the direct results for individuals of the counselling intervention have been used. In the UK, since the 1920s, congruence studies have been used to measure the achievements of guidance within the field of careers guidance. This was done by dividing people who received guidance into two groups: those who followed the advice they had been given were identified as congruent while those who did not follow the advice were identified as incongruent. The theory is that those who were congruent should prove more successful in their careers. However research showed that these congruence studies were limited as they could not cover the range of approaches and methods covered by what is known as employment counselling.[14]

Other experimental approaches to the measurement of counselling and guidance include the use of control groups. The aim here is to identify a group of unemployed people who will receive no form of intervention and to compare their progress in the search for a route back into the labour market with those who do receive counselling. There are a number of problems associated with this method: one is that it is difficult to find a group of people who receive no intervention whatsoever (as they may have informal contacts through friends and family for advice and guidance) and another is that there is a moral issue as to whether it is right to deliberately withhold services which could prove helpful to people. For this reason practitioners are themselves often unwilling to participate in such approaches to evaluation.

An interesting approach with regard to users is the tracking method (examples in Ireland, UK and Denmark) which uses follow-up information from the users to engage them more fully in the evaluation process.

Countries vary in the extent to which they have developed a culture of evaluation for counselling services. For example in Germany there is not at present a well developed methodology as to how to undertake such evaluations. The emphasis here is seen to be rather on the social, political and administrative dimensions rather than on economic calculations. In other countries, such as the UK and the Netherlands, there has been a greater emphasis in recent years on economic assessment and impact analyses. The latter examines the outcomes of counselling services and attempts to assess what would have happened had the measure not taken place. Other measurements of outcomes relate to the efficiency of services such as the cost-benefits analyses already mentioned. There are several problems with these attempts to measure the economic value of counselling:

- it is difficult to separate the impact of counselling from other interventions which may have had an influence on the person's decision-making process;

- the effects of counselling may not be visible for some time and may not be solely attributable even when that time comes;

- whose outcomes are being measured? those which fit in with what the organisation/politicians have as their main objectives or those which are tuned to what the individual wants for him/herself. (see below under Evaluate for whom?)

In some countries, for example Italy, there appears to be greater emphasis given to the evaluation of *the process* of counselling itself rather than its outcomes. This involves the ongoing monitoring of what is happening with periodic evaluations so that analysis of what is happening is undertaken and changes made as appropriate. The paragraphs later in this chapter concerning quality standards touch further on this form of evaluation.

In Spain the difference between the more quantitative analytical approach of economic and psychological assessments are contrasted with what is termed the "dialectic approach". The latter which is qualitative by nature attempts to analyse the consequences of actions in terms of social "viability" both in relation to meeting the objectives of economic performance and effectiveness and in relation to the intended social impact for the people concerned. The advantage of such methods are perceived to be that there is a chance of discovering not only the "facts" but also the significance of the various actions taken by agents participating in the counselling process. Methods used to achieve these results include interviews and focus groups. The disadvantages are that there is no allowance for the quantitative measurement of the effectiveness and efficiency of the resources used. The Spanish report points out that there are few assessments of this nature and that those which do exist are generally undertaken on the research interests of a university or academic institution.[11]

4.8.5 Evaluate for whom?

Maiello and Geroldi[12] highlight the fact that different actors involved in the counselling process may have different ideas as to what they want the process of evaluation to reveal. It is therefore important to specify for whom a counselling activity is being evaluated:

- *policy makers* are likely to be concerned with cost-benefit analysis and the measurement of outcomes; they need results which will help them to make the political arguments for counselling and develop improved labour market measures and services;

- *practitioners*, as has been noted, wish to see their work legitimized and want to learn how to improve the service which they offer;

- *the community*, may be most interested in the social benefits which the provision of counselling can bring which will entail taking a longer term view of the results which have been achieved; they will want to know whether it has helped to improve the chances of those looking for work or whether it has helped to create new work opportunities; this kind of evaluation is much less straightforward than that which measures direct and short-term quantitative outputs.

4.8.6 Setting quality standards

If quality of the counselling process itself is to be measured, and there is growing interest in this area in some countries notably the UK, then it is useful to start by defining what is implied by "quality" and what "good quality" means in real practice and establishing performance indicators to assist in its measurement.

One list of criteria on the quality of careers guidance and counselling drawn up by the Director of an evaluation centre for higher education in Denmark includes the following:

- client centredness;
- accessibility, transparency and coherence of services;
- well trained counselling staff;
- valid, precise and comprehensive information;
- referral to other counselling specialists;
- follow-up.

In the UK a national employer/industry oriented organisation, the Advice Guidance and Counselling Lead Body has almost completed standards which will set the levels of competence needed for practitioners and will act as a guarantee of quality for clients, providers and buyers of services. When completed the standards will serve as the occupational benchmark for counselling and will in all likelihood serve as the basis for the development of national qualifications as well as for performance indicators within individual providers' organisations.

Where attention to improving quality is sought in an organisation it has been proved useful to involve practitioners in undertaking much of the "evaluation" themselves: if the work is only undertaken by an external expert the practitioners may feel suspicious and negative about the process. If on the other hand the process can involve "self-directed supervision with external support" this is more likely to be successful. Clearly established performance indicators will assist practitioners to know what is expected of them and will ease the task of measurement. This kind of evaluation can form part of staff development and training.

4.8.7 *Using the results of evaluations*

The Eurocounsel research has highlighted a number of problems in usage of the results of evaluations which are undertaken. Gavira and Gonzalez[11] state boldly:

> *"the incorporation of assessment findings in the counselling process is rare and sometimes vague".*

In several countries we hear of evaluation results which are withheld because they are not favourable to the organisation concerned. This can be particularly important when an organisation is seeking funding and fears for its own future. It relates back to the reasons why evaluations are undertaken: if it is in order to measure outcomes so that the case for the future can be made then it is no wonder if unfavourable results are silenced. If on the other hand the purpose of the evaluation has been to improve the actual practice of the services offered then it of course makes no sense if the results are not published and steps taken to implement their recommendations.

4.8.8 Conclusions

One of the main debates within the area of evaluation is whether the main focus should be on quantitative measurement of outcomes or whether it is more appropriate to concentrate on qualitative aspects of the process itself so that this can be improved. The answer is that both are needed and at separate times so that the end goals of each type of evaluation (e.g. making a case to funders in the first and improving the actual service in the second) are not confused.

One of the key problems in any form of measurement of the outcomes of counselling is that counselling has not been seen as a separate labour market measure: it is generally regarded as a support to other active labour market measures such as training. Many of the evaluations which do exist are of these broader measures and it is hard to separate the results of the counselling element itself. The importance of finding objective, economic assessments of counselling is growing so that the case for counselling as a measure in its own right, as well as a support measure can be made.

The term "evaluation" is one which requires fuller explanations. As has been seen there are a number of different approaches as well as different reasons for undertaking it and different actors for whom it is undertaken. Greater clarity about this whole issue is needed so that policy makers, practitioners and researchers are clear about the purpose, methods and desired end goals of the evaluations which are undertaken. At the same time there may well be new methods and approaches to be explored with regard to this issue: one suggestion made is that the developing "social auditing" approach to measurement may be one which could be adapted to the area of measuring the economic value of counselling.

5 OVERALL CONCLUSIONS

5.1 Introduction

Chapter 2 of this report identified that creating jobs in order to tackle the high unemployment and long-term unemployment rates is seen as the top priority at present within the European Union. Counselling, in all its many guises and fulfilling varying functions, is seen as an important component of the active labour market measures currently being promoted by policy makers at European level, both to create employment in all its forms and to guard against the exclusion of growing numbers in our society. Following on from the introduction of the Delors Plan, most of the new Community Initiatives, which incorporated its ideas, include counselling and guidance as part of their provisions. It is too soon yet to evaluate the impact of the counselling and guidance component within these Initiatives but it will be useful to ensure that ongoing monitoring is in place and that full evaluations are undertaken once they have been in place for two-three years. There is a clear recognition that counselling can make active labour market measures more effective: as the OECD's Employment Outlook 1995[34] states, with regard to one of the most commonly found active labour market measures, training:

*"..the likelihood is that training programmes which are broadly targeted on the unemployed **and for which little counselling is given** will be ineffective, as evaluations in the Netherlands and the United States have shown."*

However there is no room for complacency. We are living through a period of intense change, at many different levels, and there is a need to examine what role counselling should be playing in relation to these changes and how services can be developed and improved to meet real needs. There is much more that can be done, at local, national and European levels to develop and improve the quality and effectiveness of counselling services.

5.2 Employment Growth

Job intensive growth is the current catch-phrase for what to do to solve the problem of unemployment at European level. It is well documented that traditional economic growth does not necessarily entail employment growth and a greater focus is being placed on how to ensure that the latter happens. There are two elements within this:

- the growth of new jobs and how to create them;

- equipping more people to be able to take up the jobs which exist or which are created.

For example if many new jobs are created within the high technology/high skill industries then this may do little to affect the levels of unemployment if those who are unemployed do not have the skills to meet the new demands created for labour. Counselling has a clear role in the second of these elements: it relates back to the identified function which counselling performs of matching the supply of labour with the demand. It is likely however that with the speed of developments within new technology and the rate at which systems become obsolete that counselling practitioners will need to become ever more skilled at helping their clients pursue appropriate educational and training opportunities in order to keep up with the pace of change. As has been noted in earlier Eurocounsel reports this will entail greater numbers of those who are employees as well as those who are unemployed accessing counselling services. This trend is already discernible and the concern is that those who are long-term unemployed and most disadvantaged in the labour market will become more excluded unless special efforts are made to ensure that this does not happen.

The role of counselling in relation to the creation of new jobs is less clear. As has been noted in the previous chapter, counselling practitioners in some countries believe that there is a role for counsellors to act as direct catalysts for new employment creation. Others are less certain, feeling that this will add to an already overly complex role which has to be performed and that there are other professionals, such as local economic development and community development experts whose role this should be. It may be more important for counselling practitioners to ensure that they are up to date with the existing and new opportunities for work and activity, where the evidence is that they are generally not at present, rather than to add to their many potential functions. On the other hand if more multi-disciplinary teams of counsellors are formed it may be more feasible for them to combine their knowledge and experience to identify and promote new opportunities for job creation in their local area. One of the tools which would assist them in this would be access to appropriate local labour market information.

5.3 Local labour market information

One of the recurrent themes throughout the Eurocounsel programme has been the need for counsellors to have access to more practical and recent local labour market information. Although many countries have national and regional systems in place for the compilation of statistics about the labour market and labour market trends, there is little evidence that at local level this is supplemented by up to date information about employers' needs and expectations or about developments within the intermediate labour market about which counsellors also need to be informed. Responsibility for the collation of such information, perhaps on a quarterly basis, needs to be taken at regional/local level so that it is undertaken efficiently. More important is how the information is disseminated once it is collected: one way in which this could be done would be through seminars involving counselling practitioners and other organisations concerned with the labour market from across the different sectors. This would allow practitioners to discuss the emerging trends together and it would be one way in which linkages between agencies could be seen to have practical benefits for those involved.

5.4 Long-term unemployment

The provision of counselling services for the long-term unemployed was the starting point for Eurocounsel and remains of central importance.

Over Phase 1 of the programme it was recognised that one of the ways for counselling services to help tackle the problem of long-term unemployment was to become involved before the user became unemployed for 12 months or more. In other words the preventive function of counselling was seen as one which could alleviate the problem of long-term unemployment. As more jobs have become insecure so the need for such preventive work has grown although the tendency is that only those who can pay for such services are likely to receive them (unless they belong to one of the big industries facing collapse which have made provision for their employees). This is an area where more employers, faced with impending redundancies, could consider a contribution as part of their wider social commitment to the community.

The policy paper prepared in preparation for the Council of Ministers at Essen in December 1994 made specific mention, in relation to combating long-term unemployment, of the need for "varied provision of counselling and job placement" as well as for supplementary benefits. One of the important routes out of long-term unemployment which is emerging as more flexible patterns and structures of work appear on the labour market is that of part-time and short-term contracts. As has been shown in the previous chapter there is greater likelihood that the long-term unemployed will consider these routes back into work activity if there is some support in terms of continuation of welfare benefits and secondary benefits, as has happened in Ireland. Without these supports the individual may be likely to lose more than they gain, both immediately in terms of income and in the longer term if they find themselves unemployed again and have lost the right to certain benefits.

The latest Employment in Europe report (1995)[44] produced by the European Commission reinforces the difficulties which those who are long-term unemployed are likely to have in re-entering the labour market. Employment growth alone will not solve the problem of long-term unemployment. As the report states:

"Better results [for the long-term unemployed] seem to have been achieved in cases where local circumstances and the economic situation have been allowed for and counselling appears to be essential to achieving the most effective targeting and choice of measures for individuals."

5.5 Social exclusion

Long-term unemployment is a crucial factor in the process by which individuals become socially excluded. The importance of linking social and economic policies is clearly recognised at European level and yet in many countries there is a sense that there is a growing rather than decreasing separation of economic from social policies. Economic growth, rather than employment growth, remains the key goal for many countries and unemployment is sometimes seen as the price which, unfortunately, has to be paid for competitiveness in the global market. Too many people are becoming separated completely from the labour market and in turn this leads to social exclusion or the development of an underclass. While counselling has a role to play in tackling social exclusion it is important that policy makers at European and national levels continue to press for the cohesion of social and economic policies. This will then hopefully permeate to the micro-level when action takes place. Without such an integrated approach to economic and social development it will be difficult for counselling services to do much more than patch up the problem for a few individuals.

5.6 Active citizenship

It is recognised that it is unlikely that there will be jobs for everyone, at least in the near future. It is important that the capacity for active citizenship is maintained and encouraged so that social exclusion is avoided. This active citizenship involves the empowerment of users so that they can gain real control of their own lives: this is a central element of the role counselling plays in a precarious labour market. It is allied to the need for economic measures which avoid dependency on the welfare state but which at the same time recognise the need for access to economic well-being without marginalisation and loss of quality of life.

5.7 The comprehensive counselling system

An earlier Eurocounsel report[11] designed a comprehensive counselling model which would help to cross the boundaries between what are considered to be the economic, social and educational aspects of work-related counselling. This model is repeated here because we believe that it provides a useful framework for those who are considering the development of counselling services for the future.

This diagram shows counselling services at the hub of different routes into work related activity. As well as being separate from each of these activities it is of course also the case that counselling is often an integral part of them e.g in training programmes. The central circle of counselling shown in the diagram refers to the help which individuals receive to enable them to make decisions and choices about the direction in which they are going and the path which is suited to their own circumstances. Once they have made this decision they may find further specialist help from within one of the activity circles, for example, within self-employment there will be special advisers to assist with the detail of what that person is going to do. It is within this central circle that tools such as Personal Action Planning, described in Chapter 3 of this report, are most useful. The multi-disciplinary approach, described in Chapter 4, will fit well with this comprehensive model for counselling.

The principle behind this model is that everyone should have a right not necessarily to full-time permanent employment, but to some form of work related activity, some of which earns them an income. Although the "informal economy" has not been included in the diagram it might have been as it constitutes another, and growing, element of work-related activity. One writer has described the different parts of the world of work in relation to colours: the informal economy is the "black" economy; the "mauve" economy, which consists of the small scale services provided to affluent employed members of the formal sector; and there is the "grey" economy which includes voluntary and unpaid household activities which account for a massive part of each country's unmeasured wealth. In Denmark the Users' Social Commission have advocated a more liberal interpretation of the concept of work by introducing the concept of a "Shaded Labour Market" i.e. a labour market with nuances and room for everyone to be active.[9] The counselling model which is recommended above is one which fits this notion of a wider definition of the world of work.

5.8 Training

The comprehensive counselling system implies the need both for counselling specialists and generalists. Throughout Eurocounsel the need for further professional training for counselling practitioners has been identified. The generalists in particular, who will have to be able to cross the boundaries between the economic, social and educational will need a mixture of skills in order to perform their job effectively. In some senses a new profession is emerging which has been given the provisional name of "labour field counselling" but which requires further refinement. This new profession requires recognition and to be given proper professional status. There will also be an issue about who is to provide the training for this new profession.

Even where a group of specialists are to work together in a multi-disciplinary team training will be required if they are to work effectively and to their maximum potential. Joint training between counsellors from different backgrounds (psychological, educational, economic etc.) will assist in the development of closer co-operation even where multi-disciplinary teams as such are not being established.

In addition to training, counselling practitioners require professional supervision and support. This is likely to be provided within the practitioner's own organisation but counsellors from different organisations can also usefully offer each other support and this can be one of the advantages of good linkages (see 5.11 below).

5.9 Centralisation versus decentralisation

One of the issues affecting the development of counselling services which has arisen during the course of Eurocounsel has been that of the relative merits of centralisation versus decentralisation. There are political and economic tensions involved in this debate: politically there are issues of control and accountability: in economic terms, there are resource implications as to who carries responsibility as well as issues such as the need for economies of scale. There is a general trend towards further decentralisation of services in many countries. In Italy the growth of service provision at regional and local level is accompanied by an increase in centralised control. In Ireland the new Local Employment Services are being developed to bring the delivery of service provision for the long-term unemployed closer to where the client is. Similar decentralisation and local employment services delivery are found in Spain where the development of integrated employment services (Servicio Integrado de Empleo) which involve making the best use of available public resources in an area have been tested in nine pilot areas. There is now discussion as to whether these SIPE should be extended to the whole country.[11]

While the decentralisation of service delivery is generally thought to be helpful in that it increases access to services and could perhaps facilitate greater involvement of users in the service design, there is also an argument which suggests that clearer centralised policies are required if the whole system of counselling provision is not to become totally fragmented. Such central policy-making would seek to allocate resources to the areas of greatest need and to develop a plan within which the whole framework for counselling provision within that country could be placed. We have already noted the danger that with increasing competition for resources and the growth in the "market" for counselling services there may be a tendency for the most marginalised to be excluded from services. The importance of a central approach would be to plan in such a way that everyone who has need of such services would be included at some point in the system of provision.

The main issue therefore will be to decide which elements are most usefully decentralised and which it is better to maintain centrally. The importance of central strategic planning in counselling provision is recognised. However throughout Eurocounsel the need also to plan regional level responsibility and action in labour policy development has been stressed in order to ensure that the varying needs of local labour markets are addressed.

5.10 Planning counselling services

Within the discussion about decentralisation and centralisation above, the need for strategic planning is clearly discernible. This applies to the European level, national level and regional/local policy making levels. Nationally planned services can assist in ensuring that no groups are marginalised and can set the legislative framework within which counselling provision is to take place. At regional levels there is a need to map existing provision and for key agencies to come together to plan a strategic approach to counselling provision in their area. Without such a plan it is likely that services will be duplicated and resources wasted. The process of putting such a framework in place can be beneficial itself as it brings together the different agencies and can help to form linkages if these have not previously existed. The strategic plan can indicate what form such linkages should take and how they will operate. Such a plan will assist in the effective delivery of services at local level.

5.11 Linkages

At European level there is a good example of cross sector linkages in the Standing Committee which draws together representatives from governments, the European Commission and the social partners. The need to have more linkages at national and local levels which cross the divide between the economic, social and educational has been shown to be important for the development of counselling but there is little evidence of these already existing or developing. In general it can be said that the quality of linkages needs to be improved so that they become more meaningful and less superficial.

Networking and the formation of linkages between counselling providers and between providers and other types of organisation concerned with labour market development have been shown to be an important way in which counselling services can be improved and more effective management of the labour market achieved. However there are a number of issues which have to be taken into consideration. These include the issue of who promotes such linkages as they are rarely neutral: it has been shown that where a funding body initiates them there is less likely to be a sense of equality among those participating if they are reliant on that body for their future funding. Another issue is that the benefits of linking must be clear to all: they should not be undertaken just for their own sake. The main aim of linkages should be to improve the likelihood that users will be able to progress through the different services and reach a positive outcome. Other benefits will include professional development, ease of referral and better understanding of the local labour market. One way which may assist those involved in linkages to have positive outcomes is to plan their joint action with concrete goals built in from the beginning so that they can then monitor their progress and make further plans.

Only one country, Denmark, has examples of fully integrated services between different types of organisation. Most of the other countries involved in Eurocounsel have linkages which involve the sharing of information and general communication or at most some form of general co-operation. The question which other countries will have to address, in terms of planning their services, is whether the Danish model of integration of services with their multi-disciplinary teams, is one which they would wish to and could copy. As has been noted it would appear that this model would allow for the fulfilment of the comprehensive counselling system described above but it is recognised that for many countries there may be real barriers to achieving such integration and coordination of counselling provision. Not least of these barriers is likely to be the growing market for counselling services and the competition which results from this.

5.12 The Market for Counselling

With the reduction of the monopoly of public employment services in many countries, the growing move towards the privatisation of counselling services and the increased demand for labour market related guidance for adults, a new market has appeared. One of the advantages of this trend is that a few new jobs are being created, although at the same time many are being lost from the public employment services so that the net gain is unlikely to be positive. It is too early yet to comment on what this privatisation of counselling services will mean for the quality of what is offered. The advantages can include the wider choice available to users and the fact that services may be required to demonstrate that they offer value for money. The danger is that those who cannot afford the services will be excluded. Some public bodies in the UK now provide their unemployed clients with vouchers so that they can "purchase" services from providers but a recent evaluation on the Gateways to Learning Scheme in that country which involves the use of vouchers concluded the following:

"While there was some anecdotal evidence of vouchers raising client expectations of the service our general conclusion is that vouchers failed to empower the client in the guidance market."

Coopers and Lybrand, Gateways to Learning, National Evaluation, 1994[14]

5.13 Involvement of users

The involvement of users in the planning, design and delivery of services is an area which is considered important, and indeed even to be a citizen's right as users are also tax-payers, but there is little evidence from the Eurocounsel research that there has been much user involvement to date. The European Union has a consumer protection role through the Maastricht Treaty and there is also a European Network of the Unemployed with national member organizations which inter alia represents the interests of the unemployed in relation to labour market and welfare services. The involvement of users is not just a technical issue which can lead to improved service quality, but also a political one: there is a principle of participation and involvement at stake. It is thought that more linkages of users across countries might help to serve as a catalyst to bring about changes in service provision. This is not always easy to organise however because of the transitory nature of unemployment. The various Community Initiatives described in Chapter 2 of this report could prove helpful in that they allow for transnational exchange for those involved in counselling and guidance, which could involve the users themselves.

There are examples, as have been noted in Chapter 3, where users are providing services themselves on an informal basis and this form of peer counselling is one which other countries may wish to emulate as it can both be effective and cost efficient.

In terms of meeting users' needs more effectively it has been suggested that public employment services, and other providers, should make their services available as and when the individual requests them and not based on an arbitrary time period. Although this has resource implications there are examples at present where people who have been, for example, five months unemployed are unable to access services because there is a six month unemployment criteria attached to them. This can be frustrating and demotivating for the user who has actively sought out such measures. The resource issue could perhaps be surmounted by allowing such services to be available to those who approach the provider for them while not heavily publicising this as part of the core services. Another way round this issue is to draw up a list of those most "at risk" (see Chapter 3 for a suggested list) who can access counselling services from the time they become unemployed.

5.14 The use of new technology

The rapid developments in the world of new technology are affecting and will affect the provision of counselling. The Internet has potential for future linkages between practitioners and users; for example, a new professional periodical is being planned in Denmark which will be available only through electronic format.

There is a growing range of software packages covering different information needs (occupational information, training and learning opportunities, qualifications) as well as packages which assist in the assessment of the user or help them in the decision making process. With parallel developments in communications it is likely that users will be able to access some of this information directly in their homes in the future.

Controlling the rising levels of information will be an issue for the future, both in terms of up-dating and keeping different countries' software compatible with each other. EURES (described in Chapter 2 of this report) is one example of a structure that could facilitate this process.

Access is one of the key issues for future consideration. There is a danger that a society of new technology haves and have nots is being created. Counselling providers need to ensure that full attention is given to how users can most easily access their services and whether new technology is the most appropriate tool to use in all cases. For some users it is more likely to be a barrier than a help.

5.15 Measurement and evaluation

The main purpose of measurement and evaluation should be to use the results to improve the service offered. What is apparent is that *the system* within which services operate is not often evaluated from the users' point of view, although there are some instances of this reported in the Danish and UK reports.

The research has shown that quantitative outcomes are more easily measured than qualitative aspects of the services offered. It has highlighted the need for Quality Standards in order to assist in qualitative measurements and to complement these, clear performance indicators covering both the process of counselling and how it is to be monitored and evaluated. It is recognised that this qualitative measurement will never be straightforward because of the time factor and the difficulty of separating the impact of counselling from other influences on the user.

The aim should be to establish a culture of ongoing monitoring and regular evaluation in counselling organisations which will involve practitioners and users, alongside external experts.

5.16 Resources

All the areas of counselling which have been examined require proper resourcing. This includes training for counselling practitioners, the development of linkages and the area of measurement and evaluation. Such resources will only become available at national levels if policy makers determine that this is an active labour market measure which merits fuller resourcing. At present the target set by the OECD of one hour's counselling per month for every unemployed person is out of reach in terms of the resources it would entail. However, the whole framework needs to be well resourced if it is to deliver results, especially a reduction in long-term unemployment and social exclusion.

5.17 The additional outcomes of action research

Eurocounsel has been a programme of *action* research. This has meant that as well as researching the issues surrounding counselling provision and its development, the process itself has helped to stimulate actual developments and improvements within counselling provision. These additional outcomes are substantial and wide-ranging and include the following:

- the development of linkages at local labour market level (in the areas involved in the Eurocounsel research);

- the introduction of new practices as a result of seeing what other countries are doing (following on from the successful pilot study visit programme and interim dissemination of programme results);

- the development of linkages between local labour market areas in different countries, e.g. between Ireland and Denmark;

- the use of Eurocounsel reports as training material for counselling practitioners;

- the use of Eurocounsel findings to inform policy development;

- the role of the Eurocounsel local consultant team as catalysts and consultants for the development of local and regional counselling services;

- the role of members of the Eurocounsel team in the development of counselling systems in countries where there has not been a tradition of these (e.g. Eastern and Central Europe).

Specific examples of all of these are given in Appendix 4 where the results of the action research process are analysed. In addition general dissemination of the work of Eurocounsel by the team has meant that countries as far away as Australia, Israel and Canada have benefited from this programme.

An earlier Eurocounsel report[2] pointed out that action research can involve an element of risk. It is impossible to predict the outcomes from the start and a certain element of flexibility within the research programme itself must be retained if the full benefits of such an approach are to be gained. We believe that in the case of Eurocounsel the outcomes more than justify the original decision to adopt this approach and much of this success is due to the commitment and experience of the Eurocounsel team members.

5.18 Conclusions

In the European Year for Lifelong Learning (1996) which is also the International Year for the Eradication of Poverty, it is useful to reflect on the need for opportunities for lifelong counselling: it is a key aspect of human resource development. As the labour market becomes more flexible, complex and precarious, and in the attempt to allow more people to have access to the different opportunities for work and activity, more people will find themselves moving in and out of work and between jobs than ever before. High quality counselling services are required to support individuals in their working lives and to ensure that the labour markets work as effectively as possible. At the same time counselling services have an important role to play in assisting those who are most disadvantaged to avoid social exclusion. Counselling is not the sole answer to these pressing problems of high unemployment and social exclusion, nor can it be. It does however, have a very important place within the range of measures which should be used to address these issues.

A lead in placing counselling services high on the agenda is required from policy makers at European and national levels. The final chapter of this report outlines recommendations as to how this might be achieved.

6 RECOMMENDATIONS

6.1 Summary

The Eurocounsel programme has demonstrated both the complexity and increasing importance of counselling services as an integral element of active labour market services, particularly in relation to the long-term unemployed. In most countries these services have tended to develop without any centralised planning but rather as ad hoc responses to pressures arising from changing labour markets and persistent unemployment. In some countries the provision of counselling services is increasingly being left to market forces which has the negative corollary that those who cannot afford to pay the "market" rate may be excluded from services. The complexity of provision has led to a wide variety of choice in terms of the range of services available but has also meant that services may not be as transparent as they could be for users, in terms of knowing which service to approach and what they might expect to gain from it.

Future labour market trends indicate that changing jobs and working along more flexible lines will increase. More women are entering the labour market and more men are facing unemployment. What is currently considered as "part-time work" will become more common along with short-term and temporary job contracts. These trends will have a number of implications for the provision of counselling including the following:

- people of working age will have a greater need for counselling services as they face this increased flexibility on the labour market with the more frequent job changes and altered career directions which it is likely to entail;

- the counselling services which are provided will require to be of high quality in order to meet the increasingly complex demands of users as they deal with this more flexible labour market;

- counselling services will be needed throughout a person's working life, particularly in periods of unemployment but also to prevent unemployment in handling transitions from one job to another more successfully and in seeking the appropriate skills to meet the demands of the changing labour market;

- the trend for counselling services to be offered on the open market is likely to continue and will itself have a number of implications, particularly in relation to the reinsertion of those who are marginalised within societies.

The problems of social exclusion and marginalisation are causing concern from European level to individual level. The inherent dangers of mass economic and social exclusion for the wider community are recognised: finding ways to allow people to play an active role in society is imperative. Some countries, such as Denmark, have tackled this problem by introducing activation programmes to stimulate more opportunities for people to get involved both in the labour market and in other forms of activity. Other countries are re-examining and developing social employment schemes which have been used periodically in times of high unemployment to attempt to resolve the problem of the lack of demand for labour on the market. Others are seeking to encourage employers to employ those without work by offering incentives and by subsidising the wages paid. Sometimes a mixture of several of these measures is used. However it appears that despite these attempts most countries have not completely overcome this problem. The danger is that as more counselling services are provided on the market, requiring the user to pay for them, the very people who are most in need of such services may find themselves excluded from them. Counselling, particularly a comprehensive counselling service as described in the previous chapter, has an important role to play in the reintegration of those who are economically and socially marginalised.

The purpose of this chapter is to provide recommendations for policy makers, at European, national, regional and institutional levels concerning the ways in which the effectiveness and quality of counselling services for the long-term unemployed and those at risk of becoming so can be improved and further developed. (Earlier reports of the programme have provided recommendations for improving the practice of counselling.[1, 2 & 8] The recommendations contained here are based on the findings of the whole of the Eurocounsel programme. They are broadly concerned with the need to bring economic and social policies and measures closer together, in particular as they relate to the provision of counselling. Although this integrated approach is already the stated policy of the European Union, there are ways in which countries can be encouraged to do more to put this into practice in relation to developing counselling services in a labour market context.

Clearly the different Member States of the European Union are at varying stages in the development of their counselling services and it is important that any policy recommendations which are made at European level be adapted by individual countries to suit their own circumstances. Similarly national level recommendations will require interpretation by regional and local area policy makers so that they can be amended according to local labour market needs.

6.2 European level

The importance of counselling services is inherently recognised within many of the documents and official statements of the Council of Ministers and the European Commission. However there has been no major policy statement on counselling provision in its own right. Counselling tends to be referred to as an additional element within other active labour market measures such as training rather than as a measure which can also stand alone. It is a particularly important measure as it can assist in the reinsertion not only back into the labour market but also into society, i.e. it can promote social cohesion.

The findings of the Eurocounsel programme show that the provision of counselling should be seen as a measure which can stand alone as well as one which is integral to other measures. The evidence is that stand-alone counselling services are effective both for individuals and the labour market.

- the development of counselling services, such as the Personal Action Planning approach described in Chapter 3 of this report, has already moved towards a stand-alone model focusing on the individual and all the possibilities available to them. The further recognition of counselling as a stand-alone measure will encourage the development of counselling along broad client-centred lines rather than being narrowly concerned, in different compartments, with job finding, or training, or education: such development includes the need for independent multi-dimensional counselling services e.g. the counselling houses in Denmark. It will in other words allow for the provision of the whole range of types of counselling listed in Chapter 3 of this report;

- when counselling is provided as a stand-alone service, in addition to one which is integral to other labour market measures, it becomes easier to measure and evaluate its effectiveness; as has been demonstrated in this report (Chapter 4) it is often difficult to evaluate counselling services when they are too intermingled with the labour market measure which they are supporting, for example training; it is easier to focus on the quality of what is being offered if counselling is seen to have its own remit;

- from the above it also follows that resources will be more easily targeted towards counselling services if such services are perceived to have a value and be effective in their own right.

Recommendation 1: A European level policy statement on labour market counselling

A full policy statement recognising the role of adult guidance and employment counselling as an integral and effective element of other active labour market measures (as well as a stand alone measure), is needed at European level. The statement would highlight the value of counselling in a flexible labour market with persistently high unemployment and the importance of counselling as a link between social and economic development measures. It would allow the importance of such provision to be firmly placed on the European agenda and from this further actions could be stimulated.

A policy statement could form the basis for discussions at meetings of Director Generals of Employment and Social Security and would set the foundations for policy development on counselling provision within the European Commission and within each Member State. The latter could use the statement to assist in developing a counselling element within pluriannual programmes within the European Employment Strategy. The statement should indicate the minimum standards which should be aimed for to ensure that every unemployed person has access to effective services. A suggestion for what these minimum standards might look like is made in the box below.

Suggested Minimum Standards

Every unemployed person should have access to at least one hour of counselling regarding their future work/training/educational direction on first learning that they are to be made redundant/on first becoming unemployed.

After this initial contact, unemployed people who fall into high risk categories (see Table 3 Chapter 3) should be able to access, on a voluntary basis, a further two hours of counselling assistance at any point in the first six months that they are unemployed. Access to training programmes for this high risk category should be available from three months onwards.

After six months all unemployed people should complete a full Personal Development Plan with the assistance of a qualified counselling practitioner (up to three hours of counselling assistance). This should be on a voluntary basis.

After 12 months an intensive three day counselling and motivation programme should be offered. Preferably this should be voluntary.

After 24 months a compulsory one week's counselling and confidence building sessions should be provided.

These minimum standards do not reach the target set by the OECD of one hour per month per unemployed person but they move some way towards it. The past four years' research indicates that it is important to maintain the voluntary element of the counselling provision for as long as possible. Practitioners and users have stated that the counselling effects are greater when there is no compulsion to use the service. However, the research has shown that for some of the longer-term unemployed an element of compulsion can be helpful, as it can stimulate someone who has lost all motivation to move back into some form of useful activity.

Recommendation 2:   Co-ordinate responsibility for policy on counselling within the European Commission

There is a need for improved co-ordination of policy related to labour market counselling services within the European Commission. A number of Commission services currently work on aspects of counselling policy and development including Directorates General XXII and DGV. In addition, external European bodies who have experience in this area (the European Foundation for the Improvement of Living and Working Conditions and CEDEFOP) should be involved in the co-ordinated approach to the development of policies in this area. Responsibility for this co-ordination role should be clearly allocated.

Recommendation 3: Monitoring of existing programmes and development of a new European programme specifically relating to the support and development of counselling services

One aspect of the co-ordinated approach advocated in Recommendation 2 would be to monitor what is happening within existing European activities, for example, through the various Structural Funds and Community Initiatives in relation to counselling policy, development and provision. This should be linked to on-going monitoring of developments in the Member States under their own initiative. In addition a small European programme could be established, which would focus solely on *the development* of counselling policy and provision. This programme could, for example, include the opportunity for study visits between counselling practitioners and policy makers from different countries. It would assist networking between services across national boundaries and facilitate exchange of experience and information. The programme could also include financial support to develop innovative counselling services specifically for the long-term and very long-term unemployed, which are not already covered by any of the existing Community Initiatives. For example there is a gap in provision at present in most countries for services to meet the needs of unemployed men in the 25-45 year range. The vocational counselling courses which have been designed for women returners have been shown to be innovative and extremely supportive for this group but they are not so appropriate for older men. A new approach is needed for the different categories of men who find themselves unemployed e.g. the many middle managers who have been made redundant as organisations move towards flatter structures; those with skills in traditional industries who are having to re-train; and the unskilled. There is a need for services to be developed for all of these categories and in particular for those who are in their middle or later years. Other developments which might be considered could be the innovative use of new technology for counselling provision and imaginative work linking counselling provision to activation strategies in areas where there is a low demand for labour. New technology could assist in the direct provision of European information on counselling and guidance to local areas. The development programme could aim in particular to include initiatives which are aimed at the most disadvantaged in each country - those who may find themselves excluded from the mainstream services on offer.

Recommendation 4:   A continuing role for the European Foundation for the Improvement of Living and Working Conditions in relation to research into and development of counselling services.

The European Foundation for the Improvement of Living and Working Conditions has established a wealth of research and information on counselling issues through its Eurocounsel programme. The Foundation has a continuing role to play in ensuring the dissemination of the Eurocounsel results and in undertaking further research to follow up particular aspects of the work to date. For example, it has been identified that a handbook for the measurement and evaluation of counselling services related to the labour market, based on the Eurocounsel findings could usefully be produced and disseminated across Europe. Other useful "products" would be guides and training materials for counselling practitioners on employment counselling in a changing labour market.

Recommendation 5: ***The role of the social partners at European level.***

The European organisations for employers and trade unions have an important role to play in promoting the issue of counselling and guidance at European level. The European Trade Union Congress (ETUC) and the various European employers' organisations (UNICE, CLE, CEEP) should have opportunities to work together on this issue. The subject could be included on the agenda for Social Dialogue and the social partners could be more involved in the development of the various European initiatives which include counselling and guidance. The Eurocounsel programme has shown the added value of the increased participation of employers and trade unions at all levels in the improvement of counselling services and in their increased effectiveness.

6.3   National level

Recommendation 6:   National policy statements

It is suggested that Member States could prepare a national policy statement on their own approach to the provision of counselling services, not just in public employment services but across the sectors and range of providers. This will allow each country to ensure that the framework in which counselling provision is to be set is appropriate to that country's needs. (This could form part of the pluriannual employment strategy requested in the Essen conclusions). The national statement should set out the minimum standards for that country and the main providers. It should identify any groups which the government thinks are particularly at risk of unemployment and exclusion in that country and how these groups will be targeted in terms of the counselling services they can receive. For some countries this request for a national statement will involve writing down the policy which is already in place; for others it may necessitate a fuller exercise of consultation and deliberation to determine the most appropriate approach. The statement could usefully outline the structures for provision which the country wishes to see in place, and what role other organisations, such as employers, trade unions, practitioners' and users' organisations, should be playing within these.

Recommendation 7:   The promotion of linkages

The national policy statements should aim to promote linkages between counselling providers and between them and other providers and organisations involved in labour market issues. In particular this should address the following:

- ways to foster linkages which cross the divide between provision in the economic, social and educational/training sectors;

- improving the quality of linkages (possibly by setting national guidelines as to what this might entail);

- consideration of the development of multi-disciplinary teams (involving different counselling provider organisations).

Recommendation 8: ***Improved procedures for measurement and evaluation***

At national level there is a need, where this is not already happening, for clear Quality Standards for counselling provision to be developed. These Quality Standards should, in turn, be accompanied by guidelines for the measurement and evaluation of counselling services, including qualitative as well as quantitative methods and identification of the different aims counselling organisations and their funders might have in undertaking this work; from public employment service provision to providers in the non-government and private sector.

Recommendation 9: ***The importance of welfare benefits linked to counselling***

One of the important tangential issues emerging from the Eurocounsel national reports which should be considered alongside the development of counselling services, is that of welfare benefits for the long-term unemployed who are considering taking up short-term or part-time work. As has been seen, dependence on welfare and associated benefits can act as a barrier to reintegration into the labour market, as people may lose financially in the short term if the wage which is proposed does not match the benefits they are receiving (more often a problem for married men with children whose benefits are higher) or if the job is only temporary they run the risk of losing their eligibility for certain benefits if they find themselves out of work again. This is known as the unemployment trap. At the same time this problem can make the job of the counselling practitioner more difficult as it may be harder to assist the client to chose a route back into employment or training if such a situation exists. In order to make counselling services as effective as possible it is important to consider all policies affecting reintegration as a total package to support the individual's return to the labour market.

Recommendation 10:   The involvement of employers

At national and local levels companies and employers could become more involved in the development of counselling services. A number of ways have been suggested in this report. These include the following:

- the involvement of employers in the development of effective and accurate labour market information (see below);

- pro-active encouragement to all employers to consider the recruitment of long-term unemployed people; this could take the form of subsidies but would more importantly include some form of training/education/support for employers to help them overcome any negative perceptions or experience they may have; they could then be directly involved in guaranteed job interview schemes (where employers contract to offer interviews to long-term unemployed people) offering work placements and other schemes to assist the long-term unemployed;

- offering counselling to those who are being made redundant; in particular, small and medium-sized enterprises could be encouraged to adopt this approach already found in many large scale companies, possibly through collaboration at regional level with the support of employers' organisations. During the Eurocounsel programme many successful initiatives of pre-redundancy counselling within companies were identified.

Recommendation 11: ***The involvement of trade unions***

Trade unions have increasingly recognised the importance of counselling as an active labour market measure. However, as the labour market changes, unions will have to consider how to develop their services in this area. The future labour market will involve more people changing their jobs several times in their career and more people working flexibly. Constant upskilling and learning will be important for survival in this developing labour market. The Year of Lifelong Learning (1996) demonstrates the importance attached to this concept at European level. In addition to lifelong learning there will be a need for "lifelong counselling" to assist people through the intricacies of the world of work and training.

The unions face a challenge in responding to these changes and meeting the altered needs of their members: they may wish as part of their overall strategic thinking to consider what their role should be in the development of counselling services. One area that has been suggested is to consider involvement in the development of new services for example such as those targeted on men aged 35-55. The role which trade unions in some companies play in pre-redundancy counselling, in advising on continuing training and other schemes available and in negotiation with employers to improve in-company policies in this area is one which can offer a model for other trade unions. There is also a role for trade unions in developing local labour market information and in working with counselling services to improve access to and quality of provision.

Recommendation 12: *Improving local labour market information*

One of the key tools which a counselling practitioner requires is up to date, accurate and useable local labour market information. Without this information, even the basic goal of matching the supply and demand for labour cannot be achieved adequately and the more complex understanding of the flexible labour market will not be reached. Throughout the Eurocounsel programme the lack of adequate local labour market information has been highlighted and has been identified in all the countries participating in the programme as an issue. The problem is not that the statistics are not collected but that the interpretation of the statistics is not easily available and tends not to be accompanied by up to date qualitative information about a particular local labour market area. This is an issue which has to be tackled country by country and the national policy framework may wish to detail how this need is to be met. Most countries will undoubtedly consider that this is an area already covered as there are usually national bodies involved in the collection of labour market statistics: but the evidence from Eurocounsel is clear that labour market information tends not to be in a form which is readily accessible to those who have to use it at local level. If national guidelines as to how this could be achieved, according to each country's own circumstances, are established then it will be easier to allocate the responsibility for interpreting, producing and disseminating the information at local level. In turn this should enable improvements to be made to regional, national and European level labour market information, with the emphasis being on accessibility and practicality.

6.4 Regional and local levels

Recommendation 13: Regional strategies and local action plans

It is proposed that one element of each national policy statement would be to require each regional labour market area in the country to prepare a strategic plan for the provision of counselling in that area, set within the overall national strategic framework. The first step to putting such a regional strategy in place would be to map the existing provision in the area (if this had not already been done) so that a clear picture of the strengths and weaknesses of what is in place can be prepared. The key providers should then come together so that they can discuss existing provision and ways in which they think it should develop. (The process would be similar to that used in Phase 1 of Eurocounsel which is described in the Phase 1 synthesis report[2]) It is recognised that the situation will vary between countries and between local and regional areas: some countries have already elements of this approach in place.

The regional strategies would cover issues such as the following:

- the funding of services;
- linkages: which organisations would be involved and how the linkages would be developed and maintained;
- identify any gaps which have to be met;
- examine ways in which services can work more closely together e.g. between those involved in self-employment counselling/small business development and those involved in employment counselling/educational guidance; this could include ideas for cross-organisation training (see below);
- training of practitioners.

The regional strategy would then be used to plan action at local labour market level, always allowing for flexibility to respond to varying local circumstances.

In drawing up the regional strategy it will be useful for those responsible to refer to the recommendations made at the end of each of the country reports for Phase 3 of the Eurocounsel programme. Although many of the issues raised will be of interest to more than one country, some of them are country specific. The kinds of recommendations which have been made (not already included in this Chapter) are summarised under main topic areas in Appendix 5.

Recommendation 14: *Training for counselling practitioners*

The job of the counselling practitioner is a developing one: as more comprehensive services are developed which cross over the traditional boundaries between careers guidance, employment counselling and other forms of advice and information provision linked to the labour market and the individual's route towards it, so the role of the professional involved in this provision becomes more complex. A counsellor may still specialise in one of the traditional areas listed above but increasingly will have to be able to understand the rest of what is offered. (This will also be in their own interest as there will be more job opportunities for the counselling practitioner who can move between the different specialisms than for the person who is confined to one area alone. There is evidence that this movement between the different specialisms of counselling is beginning to happen in some countries such as Denmark, the UK and outside the EU, in Canada.)

The Eurocounsel programme has shown that a new profession, which crosses over the traditional counselling areas of employment counselling, career guidance and self-employment/small business development is emerging. This new profession will require its own training with official recognition: those who undertake such courses could be trained as generalists who can assist users with all their work related requirements or may still be trained as specialists but with broader understanding of the other areas of counselling available. Many of those who are already trained in one of the discrete disciplines may need to take additional short courses to add to their existing expertise:

for others coming into the profession a newly designed qualification which brings the different elements together will be required. The national policy statement could be the appropriate level at which the decision is taken as to who will undertake this course development so that there are nationally recognised standards. This will ensure that the profession is given the status it requires to attract quality recruits.

Training for counselling practitioners should be ongoing as part of their professional development. It is partly the responsibility of management in individual organisations to implement training development but the regional strategy can also make suggestions to facilitate cross-organisational training and development. For example, as has been suggested, a regional strategy might include a model for the dissemination of effective and up to date labour market information among different organisations through the medium of a seminar or forum to which several organisations could be invited allowing practitioners to share their understanding of the issues.

Illustrated below are some of the proposals put forward for training development in the individual national reports from the Eurocounsel programme.

TRAINING

- to promote a readiness to be innovative and undertake proactive work on the part of counselling services, counsellors should be confronted now and again with points of view contrasting distinctly with the self-evident nature of their own work; this should involve study visits and seminar programmes; (Germany)

- there is a need for staff development across disciplines and sectors; (United Kingdom; Denmark)

- counsellors must be able to understand the changes that are affecting the economic and social system so that they can make their clients aware of the changeable nature of the labour market; (Italy)

- both general as well as specialist training is needed; (Spain)

- training for counsellors should include a knowledge of entrepreneurship and its requirements; (Denmark)

- there is a need for professionalisation and up-grading of qualifications of counsellors; too many see it as an educational/social concept rather than one linked to vocationally oriented economic development. (Denmark)

Recommendation 15: ***The development of new technology within counselling provision***

Appropriate uses of new technology within counselling provision should be further developed. The aim should be to reduce counselling practitioners' time on non-essential tasks so that they are able to devote as much time as possible to client contact and the development and improvement of the services they offer. Software is already well developed to undertake a range of assessment and analytical techniques with clients. New technology can be further developed to assist in information dissemination (for clients and for counselling practitioners themselves), in client record-keeping and tracking and in general monitoring of service provision. In addition, new technology will be able to assist linkages between providers and with other organisations involved in labour market issues.

6.5 Conclusion

The Eurocounsel programme has analysed ongoing developments in the area of counselling provision linked to the changing labour market. Those who are long-term unemployed have much to gain from such services as they can play a crucial role in economic and social reintegration. However there is a need to ensure that services are accessible to this group, of a high quality and that they are properly resourced. At the same time it is recognised that as the labour market becomes more flexible the demands it makes on individuals increase and there is a growing need for counselling services to be available, when needed, throughout a person's working life. There is much that can be done at European policy-making level to promote and support the further development of counselling provision and to encourage individual countries and local areas to take appropriate action. This action research programme has begun a process of development and improvement - of access to and the process and outcomes of labour market counselling - but it is only a very small first step. Much remains to be done if the potential of these services to contribute to the prevention and reduction of unemployment and social exclusion is to be realised.

Appendix 1

THE EUROCOUNSEL TEAM

| Local Consultants |

1 Petra Draxl (Austria) (participated in Phase 2)
   ÖSB Unternehmensberatung GmbH
   Neubaugasse 31
   A-1070 Vienna

2 Lina Gavira and Francisco Gonzalez (Spain)
   GEISE S.L.
   Divina Pastora 45
   41005 Sevilla

3 Fred van Gunst (Netherlands) (participated in Phase 3)
   Centaur Onderzoek & Advies
   van Diemenstraat, 410
   NL - 1001 EC Amsterdam

4 Norma Hurley (UK)
   Blake Stevenson Ltd
   12/a Cumberland Street South East Lane
   UK - Edinburgh EH3 6RU
   Scotland

5   Marco Maiello and Gianni Geroldi (Italy)
    Fondazione Seveso
    Viale Tunisia 2
    I-20124 Milan

6   Peter Plant (Denmark)
    Royal Danish School of Educational Studies
    Margrethevej 3
    DK-2960 Rungsted Kyst
    Denmark

7   Jürgen Schumacher and Karin Stiehr (Germany)
    Institut für Soziale Infrastruktur
    Nonnenpfad 14
    60599 Frankfurt

8   Jean-Paul Villie (France) (participated in Phase 3)
    Sitelle
    2, place de la Mairie
    F - 42570 Saint-Héand

Co-ordinator

Glenys Watt
Blake Stevenson Ltd
12/A Cumberland Street South East Lane
UK - Edinburgh EH3 6RU

Research Manager

Wendy O'Conghaile

European Foundation for the Improvement of Living and Working Conditions

Wyattville Road

Louglinstown

Co. Dublin

Ireland

Advisory Committee Members

A list of those who have participated in the Eurocounsel Advisory Committee 1991-1995

Employers

Xenophon Constantinidis

Bernard Le Marchand

Trade Unions

Paolo Adurno

Joano Agudo

Maria Helena Andre

Governments

Stanley King

Marinos Sarivalassis

Andrew Scott

Achim Wittrock

Gary Watson

European Commission

Danny Brennan	) DGV
Rita Veiga da Cunha	) DGXXII
Panayotis Sigonis	) DGV
Jackie Morin	) DGV

Committee of Experts of EFILWC

Bill Daniel

I.L.O.

Sergio Ricca

OECD

Donald McBain

Appendix 2

REFERENCE

1 Counselling - A Tool for the Prevention and Solution of Unemployment: Eurocounsel Synthesis Final Report Phase 2, by Glenys Watt
Luxembourg: Office for Official Publications of the European Communities, 1994 (Available in EN, FR, DE, IT, ES, DA)

2. Counselling and Long-Term Unemployment : Report on Phase 1 of the Eurocounsel Action Research Programme, by Glenys Watt
Luxembourg: Office for Official Publications of the European Communities, 1992 (Available in EN, FR, DE, IT, ES, DA)

3 Counselling and Long-Term Unemployment : Report on Phase 1 of the Eurocounsel Action Research Programme, Executive Summary by Glenys Watt
Dublin: European Foundation for the Improvement of Living and Working Conditions, 1992 (available in all EU working languages)

4 Counselling for the Unemployed : Issues for Policy Makers, By Glenys Watt
Dublin: European Foundation for the Improvement of Living and Working Conditions, 1991 (Working Paper: available in all EU working languages)

5   Counselling for the Unemployed : Issues for Practitioners, by Glenys Watt
Dublin: European Foundation for the Improvement of Living and Working Conditions, 1991 (Working Paper: available in all EU working languages)

6   Seminar for Senior Public Employment Service Officials : Edinburgh 25 - 27 January 1993
Working Paper by Glenys Watt, Dublin: European Foundation for the Improvement of Living and Working Conditions, 1993

7   Eurocounsel Case Study Portfolio : Examples of Innovative Practice in Labour Market Counselling, by Norma Hurley
Luxembourg: Office for Official Publications of the European Communities, 1994

8   A Guide to Good Practice in Labour Market Counselling, by Glenys Watt
Luxembourg: Office for Official Publications of the European Communities, 1994

9   Counselling Services Responding to a Changing Labour Market : Eurocounsel Phase 3 Report, Denmark, by Peter Plant
Dublin: European Foundation for the Improvement of Living and Working Conditions, 1995 (Working Paper in EN, DA)

10 Eurocounsel Phase 3 Final Report, Germany, by Karin Stiehr and Jürgen Schumacher
Dublin: European Foundation for the Improvement of Living and Working Conditions, 1995 (Working Paper in EN, DE)

11 Eurocounsel Phase 3 Report, Spain, By Lina Gavira and Francisco Gonzalez
Dublin: European Foundation for the Improvement of Living and Working Conditions, 1995 (Working Paper in EN, ES)

12 Eurocounsel Phase 3 Report, Italy, by Marco Maiello and Gianni Geroldi
Dublin: European Foundation for the Improvement of Living and Working Conditions, 1995 (Working Paper in EN, IT)

13 Developing Labour Market Services for the Contemporary Labour Market : Eurocounsel Phase 3 Report, Ireland, by Tom Ronayne, Phyllis Murphy and Carmel Corrigan
Dublin: European Foundation for the Improvement of Living and Working Conditions, 1995 (Working Paper)

14 Counselling Responses to the Changing Labour Market in the 1990s : Eurocounsel Phase 3 Report, United Kingdom, by Norma Hurley
Dublin: European Foundation for the Improvement of Living and Working Conditions, 1995 (Working Paper)

15   Eurocounsel Report, France, by Jean-Paul Villié
     Dublin: European Foundation for the Improvement of Living and Working Conditions, 1995 (Working Paper)

16   Eurocounsel Report, Netherlands, by Fred van Gunst
     Dublin: European Foundation for the Improvement of Living and Working Conditions, 1995 (Working Paper)

17   Denmark: Eurocounsel Phase 2 Final Report, by Peter Plant. European Foundation for the Improvement of Living and Working Conditions, 1993. (Available in English and Danish).

18   Germany: Counselling and long-term unemployment: Eurocounsel - Phase 2 Final Report for Germany, by Jürgen Schumacher and Karin Stiehr. European Foundation for the Improvement of Living and Working Conditions, 1993. (Available in English and German).

19   Ireland: Eurocounsel - Phase 2 Final Report, by Carmel Duggan and Tom Ronayne. European Foundation for the Improvement of Living and Working Conditions, 1993. (Available in English).

20   Italy: Eurocounsel - Phase 2 Final Report, by Gianni Geroldi and Marco Maeillo. European Foundation for the Improvement of Living and Working Conditions, 1993. (Available in English and Italian).

21	Spain: Eurocounsel - Phase 2 Final Report, by Lina Gavira and Francisco Gonzales. European Foundation for the Improvement of Living and Working Conditions, 1993. (Available in English and Spanish).

22	United Kingdom: Eurocounsel - Phase 2 Final Report by Rita Griffiths. European Foundation for the Improvement of Living and Working Conditions, 1993. (Available in English).

23	Public Welfare Services and Social Exclusion : The Development of Consumer-Oriented Initiatives in the European Union, by Nicholas Deakin, Ann Davis, Neil Thomas
Luxembourg: Office for Official Publications of the European Communities, 1995

24	Local Community Action and Social Policy, a Discussion Document, by Gabriel Chanan
Luxembourg: Office for Official Publications of the European Communities, 1993

25	White Paper on European Social Policy : A Way Forward for the Union
Luxembourg: Office for Official Publications of the European Communities, 1994

26	Jobs Study 1950 - 1995
Paris, OECD, 1994

27 Les syndicats face à l'exclusion et aux précarités sociales : Bilan des actions de la Confédération Européene des Syndicats et de ses Organisations, by G. Fonteneau and A. Meunier
CES, 1994

28 The Age of Unreason, by Charles Handy
Century, April 1991

29 Combating Social Exclusion in the European Union
Anti-Poverty Group, 1995

30 World Employment 1995
ILO, Geneva, 1995

31 ERGO I Final Report Phase I
Commission of the European Communities, Brussels, 1992

32 Vocational Counselling Provision for Women in the European Union, by Kyra Veniopoulou
European Commission, DGV, April 1995

33 Educational and Vocational Guidance in the European Community : Synthesis Report
Commission of the European Communities, Brussels, 1993

34 Employment Outlook, 1995
Paris, OECD, July 1995

35 White Paper on Growth, Competitiveness and Employment
Commission of the European Communities, Brussels
Luxembourg: Office for Official Publications of the European
Communities, 1994

36 Essen Summit : Conclusions of the Presidency; Bulletin of the European Union, 1994

37 Medium Term Social Action Programme, (1995 - 97)
Communication from the Commission to the Council, the European Parliament, the Economic and Social Committee and the Committee of the Regions, April 1995

38 Bridging the Gulf, Improving social cohesion in Europe : the work of the European Foundation for the Improvement of Living and Working Conditions, 1984 - 1993, by Colin Ball
Luxembourg: Office for Official Publications of the European Communities, 1994

39 Business and Social Exclusion, A Guide to Good Practice by John Griffiths. A Report to the London Enterprise Agency for Bsuiness and Social Exclusion Conference, 11 - 12 May 19954. Sponsored by British Telecom

40 Reorganisation der Arbeitsmarktpolitik, by Schmid, Berlin, 1994

41 Flexibility and Organisation, Report of Expert Working Group. Executive Summary by Professor Dr Gerhard Bosch
European Commission, 1995

42 Older Workers and Labour Market Programmes and Policies in the European Union, by Elizabeth Drury
Dublin: European Foundation for the Improvement of Living and Working Conditions, July 1995 (Working Paper)

43 Investing in Ageing Workers - a Framework for Analysing Good Practice in Europe by Alan Walker
Dublin: European Foundation for the Improvement of Living and Working Conditions, 1995 (Working Paper)

44 Employment in Europe, 1995
Luxembourg: Office for Official Publications of the European Communities, 1995

45 Europe and the Global Information Society : Recommendations to the European Council by members of the High-Level Group on the Information Society, Brussels, May 1994

46 Interim Report of the Task Force on Long-term Unemployment
Dublin: Government of Ireland, 1995

47 Leonardo da Vinci Programme, Vademecum
European Commission, Directorate General XXII, Education, Training and Youth

48 The Economic Value of Careers Giudance, by Killeen, White and Watts
London: Policy Studies Institute in association with *National Institute for Careers Education and Counselling, 1992*

49 Vocational Guidance and Counselling for Adults. Summary Report on the Services available for the Unemployed and especially the Long-term Unemployed.
CEDEFOP, 1990 (available in DE, EN, FR)
Luxembourg: Office for Official Publications of the European Communities

50 Transnational Vocational Guidance and Training for Young People and Adults.
CEDEFOP, 1990 (available in DE, EN, FR)
Luxembourg: Office for Official Publications of the European Communities

51 Transnational Vocational Guidance and Training for Young People and Adults. Synthesis Report of Eight Studies.
CEDEFOP, 1990
Luxembourg: Office for Official Publications of the European Communities

52 Occupational Profiles of Vocational Counsellors in the European Community: A Synthesis Report.
Luxembourg: Office for Official Publications of the European Communities, 1992

Appendix 3

Definitions

There are many terms used in the English language for counselling and guidance for adults in relation to the labour market. Many of the terms have their own distinct meaning but are also used rather loosely by people who wish to denote the general kinds of services available for unemployed adults. The terms include "career guidance", "employment counselling", "vocational guidance or counselling", "advice" and "information". As has been seen in an earlier Eurocounsel report this plethora of names for the activity under consideration is not shared by all languages (cf Eurocounsel Report Phase 1). Within the English language some of the terms are used more frequently in certain situations than in others. For example "careers guidance" is commonly referred to when dealing with school and college students who are deciding in which direction they want to aim for the future: it is a term that many unemployed people consider inappropriate as they struggle to find any job at all let alone something as grand as a career.

During the Eurocounsel programme the term "counselling" has been used as a catch-all word to include:

- information giving;
- guidance;
- advice;
- and counselling itself.

Information giving is the most commonly found activity by those who offer "counselling" for the unemployed. It consists of many different kinds of information including information about the labour market and job opportunities, information about labour market programmes and information about educational and training opportunities and welfare support. It can be delivered in a variety of ways including printed materials, the use of television and radio and increasingly the use of new technology.

Guidance is often part of a phrase such as "career guidance" or "vocational guidance". It is used to denote a sense of steering and giving direction and tends to be undertaken in more formal educational settings.

Advice on the other hand denotes a less formal activity. It concerns offering a possible solution or course of action to the client which they may or may not decide to follow.

Counselling per se is less commonly found where it denotes a sense of empowerment of the individual who is enabled through the process of counselling to make decisions about the future on their own behalf. One of the reasons why this is less frequent is because it requires an adequate allocation of time which in turn implies greater resources which many organisations involved in these activities simply do not possess.

A useful definition of the kinds of counselling to which we are referring in the Eurocounsel programme is given in a recent report on Vocational Counselling Provision for Women in the EU (April 1995)[32]:

> *"..counselling encompasses all the forms of structured provision of advice, support and information through which an individual arrives at an informed and self-responsible understanding on how to tackle their work-related circumstances."*

Appendix 4

Results of the action element of the Eurocounsel programme

The local consultants who have participated in the Eurocounsel programme have all been active in the action part of the Eurocounsel programme as well as in the research element. In order to assess exactly what this has meant in practical terms each local consultant was asked to complete a questionnaire detailing their activities with regard to:

- dissemination at conferences and workshops, training, and printed material;
- consultancy assignments;
- developments in local services as a result of the programme; and
- influence on policy development which can be attributed directly to Eurocounsel.

The results of this survey have been analysed and are summarised here.

General results

Overall the impact of the programme has been high. It has resulted in greater recognition for the importance of counselling in relation to the labour market and to meeting the needs of those who are long-term unemployed or at risk of being so.

At local level, where much of the research has been undertaken, there is evidence that there is generally a better understanding of counselling issues and in several instances better local co-ordination of counselling services.

Detailed results

Inspiration from other countries facing similar problems

There are several examples within the survey of countries which have been inspired by what is happening in other countries. e.g.

- Denmark has been inspired by examples of regional development from Italy and Ireland.
- UK inspired by examples of strategic co-ordination by Denmark.

- Israel now examining the introduction of a Danish style job and training rotation scheme after a presentation by the Danish local consultant.

Eurocounsel material used for training counsellors

There are examples of Eurocounsel materials being incorporated into the training of counselling practitioners in Italy, Germany, Ireland and Denmark.

Policy development

In Ireland the Eurocounsel documentation has been used by the Task Force on Long-term Unemployment to assist in the policy development of services for the long-term unemployed and in the development of the new Local Employment Service.

In Italy, the proposed reform of labour market policies in Friuli Venezia Giulia has been based on Eurocounsel.

Development of local counselling services

Local action plans developed in Badalona and Campina de Sevilla (Spain) involving users, practitioners, municipal and provincial authorities and social partners.

Other examples of the development of local counselling services come from Tallaght (Ireland) and Lombardy (Italy).

Development of new counselling systems

At national level, the Eurocounsel co-ordinator was involved in the design and development of the new occupational and counselling services in the Czech Republic.

In Carmona and El Viso, Sevilla, Spain a new system (AMPI, Accion Metodologica Piloto de Insercion) which focuses on an integrated and participative approach with a strong emphasis on networking, has been developed by the Spanish local consultants with funding from the Andalusian Labour Ministry.

Dissemination

The dissemination of the results of Eurocounsel has been wide-reaching through the forms of conferences, seminars and printed materials. In addition to the participating countries there have been presentations in:

- Portugal;
- Austria;
- Sweden;
- Belgium;
- Hungary;
- Czech and Slovak Republics;
- Israel;
- Canada;
- Australia.

In Spain dissemination has also taken place through the media of radio and television.

Independent study trips have been organised involving practitioners and policy makers from the UK, Denmark and Ireland.

Appendix 5

RECOMMENDATIONS FOR REGIONAL AND LOCAL STRATEGIES

- Opportunities for work and activity in a changing labour market;
- Linkages;
- The evaluation and measurement of counselling services;
- General issues.

COUNSELLING IN RELATION TO OPPORTUNITIES FOR WORK AND ACTIVITY IN A CHANGING LABOUR MARKET

- counselling services should seek to involve those already working in the wider range of work and activity opportunities such as employers, trainers and work placement providers, in order to use their experiences to be able to cover all opportunities on the labour market with clients. This involvement could include presentations directly to clients or sessions with counsellors to provide them with fuller information; (Germany)

- the opportunities available may not be the ideal work which the unemployed person is seeking: this increases the importance of after-care services for clients and highlights the need for services not just for the unemployed but also for those who find themselves in more precarious forms of employment and activity; (Germany)

- counsellors should be able to advise on the full range of opportunities for work and activity; (Denmark)

- counselling in a changing labour market needs to be multi-dimensional and holistic not one-dimensional and lineal; it is particularly important to develop the client's ability to take control for themselves and to learn how to handle change; (Spain)

- counsellors should be in a position to help their clients assess the risks inherent in the flexible labour market and how to deal with them: e.g. the risks of de-skilling, of progressive marginalisation and of dependence on protected work; (Italy; Ireland; Germany)

- some provision for migrant workers and returning emigrants is needed; this could be undertaken by co-operation between counselling services and country-specific organisations and associations for migrants; (Germany)

- counselling services should develop ways in which to assist unemployed people involved in the informal economy to move to the formal economy; (United Kingdom)

- counsellors should be catalysts of job creation opportunities by acting as mediators and brokers between their clients and employers or job creation agents; (Italy)

- counselling should support local economic development initiatives in an active back-up role e.g. through better links between local training efforts and job creation; (Denmark)

- there is a need for more and improved technical and economic resources for the development of counselling; in particular there is a need for systematic and comprehensive counselling in all the alternative opportunity areas for work and activity; (Spain)

- counselling services need to embrace a role with regard to the achievement of equity i.e. to ensure that all people have access to information/counselling services and that some groups are not excluded; (Ireland)

- the need for a comprehensive national system; (Ireland)

LINKAGES

- there is a need for collaboration and dialogue between local authority policy decision makers and counselling services, so that objectives are clearly set out as well as forms and efficiency of work; (Germany)

- there is a need for greater contact between counselling services and other organisations in the field of labour market policy; counselling services should consider to what extent they can make employers and trade unions attractive offers of their services as it is recognised that the existence of mutual benefits helps linkages to work well; (Germany)

- local authority officials and those working in municipalities to be trained to act as additional suppliers of some services e.g. by providing information which is commonly sought and thereby reducing the pressure on time for counsellors themselves to allow them to focus in more depth on guidance and counselling; (Germany)

- the need for follow-through of clients between different agencies; (United Kingdom)

- the need for an agreed Action Plan in a local area to give coherence to the counselling provision: this should enable vertical rather than horizontal progression for the client to occur; (United Kingdom)

- counselling services should help people to avoid becoming trapped in a weak position in the labour market; (Ireland)

- the need to expand links with local employers through a strategic approach to linkages at regional level; (United Kingdom)

- the need for a more formalised system of linkages: horizontal and vertical; between statutory and non-statutory; between services providers and government departments etc.; (Ireland)

- the development of linkages between the economic and social i.e. between counselling for the primary labour market, counselling for education/training, counselling for social employment, for business and self-employment development and for individual welfare; (United Kingdom; Denmark; Spain)

- counselling bodies need to adopt networking models internally as well as externally e.g. to encourage integrated communication within their own organisation; (Denmark; United Kingdom)

- counselling bodies should co-operate in joint service provision where possible for example, in multi-disciplinary counselling centres; (Denmark)

EVALUATION AND MEASUREMENT OF COUNSELLING SERVICES

- a local strategy should set the minimum standards for counselling provision; (United Kingdom)

- evaluation should be conducted in relation to specific regional contexts; (Italy)

- users should be involved in developing, monitoring and evaluating services; (Spain, Italy, Ireland)

- the need for a comprehensive evaluation of some of the more recent initiatives for the long-term unemployed (which all include some level of provision in relation to counselling and guidance) e.g. the Back to Work Allowance Scheme; the newly created pilot National Guidance Service for Adults. This should be done before taking major decisions in relation to service development; (Ireland)

- in relation to measurement it must be remembered that the economic yardstick is one-dimensional: counselling is a multi-dimensional intervention and needs to include ethical considerations in its measurement; (Denmark)

GENERAL

Tuning the service to the client's needs

- the need to attune the counselling service more to the individual requirements of those seeking advice. For example the needs in western and eastern Germany are very different: put simply, in the western part of the country there is a tendency for counsellors to underestimate the individual's capacity to act while this tends to be over-estimated in eastern Germany; (Germany)

- clients should know what to expect from counselling in a clearly displayed statement on the premises; (United Kingdom)

- counselling services should be clearly signposted both literally and metaphorically; (Denmark)

- longer and more in-depth counselling should be available on a one to one basis for those individuals who need it (based on the identified high risk groups p.34); (United Kingdom)

- the importance of longitudinal methods for special needs groups which will involve more expensive, extensive methods for those with more difficult situations; (Spain)

Relating to general counselling services

- there are deficiencies in the operation of information services; (Ireland)

- counselling services should be pro-active and not just reactive e.g. should develop outreach work. (Denmark)

European Foundation for the Improvement of Living and Working Conditions

THE ROLE OF ADULT GUIDANCE AND EMPLOYMENT COUNSELLING IN A CHANGING LABOUR MARKET
Final Report on
Eurocounsel: An Action Research Programme on Counselling and Long-Term Unemployment

Luxembourg: Office for Official Publications of the European Communities

1996 – 212pp. – 16 x 23.5cm

ISBN 92-827-8279-4

Price (excluding VAT) in Luxembourg: ECU 21.50